THE SUBSTANCE OF GOTHIC

THE SUBSTANCE
OF GOTHIC

Six Lectures on the Development
of Architecture from
Charlemagne to
Henry VIII

GIVEN AT THE LOWELL INSTITUTE, BOSTON
IN NOVEMBER AND DECEMBER, 1916

By

RALPH ADAMS CRAM
LITT.D., LL.D., F.A.I.A., F.R.G.S., ETC.

BOSTON
MARSHALL JONES COMPANY
MDCCCCXVII

PRINTED BY
THE UNIVERSITY PRESS, CAMBRIDGE, U. S. A.

PREFACE

In philosophical terminology every existing thing is composed of substance and accidents, the first being its essential quality, the
second its visible form. Accidents may
change while the substance remains immutable, and the substance may change though
the accidents remain as before. Between
the cradle and the grave man goes through
a constant process of change, but that which
makes each a definite individual, marked
off from all others of his race in unique
individuality, remains a fixed and immutable ego, however much it may develop
and expand, or degenerate and fail. Death
itself, which destroys the accidents of
earthly housing, cannot touch the immortal
soul or diminish its integrity, though the
visible manifestation may differ as much
from that of its earthly habitation as the
moth differs from the chrysalis or the antecedent worm. So in the case of the Holy
Sacrament of the Altar, the words of con-

secration and the miracle that follows
thereon have no effect on the accidents of
form, shape, colour, ponderability, but the
substance has been wholly changed, and
though to the senses the wafer is still but
a white disk of unleavened bread, the wine
but the fermented juice of the grape, the
one has become, *in substance,* the very Body
of Christ, the other His sacred Blood.

For four centuries and more it has been
the fashion to deny this fundamental difference between substance and accidents, to
maintain that the accidents are in fact the
substance itself, and perilously to confuse,
in every category of thought and action, the
essential " thing in itself," with the casual
and transient forms of its manifestations.
The war is at the same time the penalty of
this folly and its drastic corrective. Whatever may be its issue, one thing is sure, and
that is its operation towards breaking all
things into their component parts of inner
fact and outward appearance: its merciful
revelation of the illusory nature of the visible forms of the commonly accepted dogmas and axioms of four centuries, and of
the eternal verity of things long hidden
under deceitful masks, of the eternal falsity

of things that had come before us in appealing and ingratiating guise.

I have called these lectures, given during the winter of 1916–17 in the Lowell Institute course in Boston, "The Substance of Gothic," because in them an effort is made, though briefly and superficially, to deal with the development of Christian architecture from Charlemagne to Henry VIII, rather in relation to its substance than its accidents; to consider it as a definite and growing organism and as the exact and unescapable exponent of a system of life and thought antipodal to that of the modernism that began its final dissolution at the beginning of August A.D. 1914, rather than in the light of its accidents of form and ornament and details of structural design. Art was always the expression of the best in any people and in any time, until the last generation when, if we are to retain any belief that then there was a definite "best," we must hold that it changed its nature and became, if not the manifestation of the worst, at least that of a very low average. During the period with which I deal there is no question on this point; between the fall of Rome and the triumph of the Renaissance art of every kind was a visible setting forth of the highest aspirations and capacities of men, and it was even more intimately a part of personal and communal life than ever before. In every particular of ideal and of execution it follows precisely from life, and is neither to be estimated nor understood except in its relation to this life which itself must first be estimated and understood if its art is to be apprehended except after a very superficial fashion.

When, early in the last century, men began to think back into the Middle Ages, the approach was invariably made through what philosophy would call the accidents of a time and a life that had left us no more than their superficial records. The admiration that grew so rapidly was not for the substance of Mediævalism, for scholastic or sacramental philosophy, for Catholic theology, for communal organization on a human scale, it was rather for the outward forms of the several Christian arts, for the ceremonial and the devotional material of religion, for the insubstantial residuum of an ultra-mystical philosophy, for the poetry and charm and pageantry of the Mediæval decadence. It has needed this war to drive men back and beyond the form to the matter itself, and to give them some realization of the singular force and potency and right- eousness of an epoch which begins now to show itself as the best man has ever created, and one as well that contains within itself the solution of our manifold and tragical difficulties, and is in fact the model whereon we must rebuild the fabric of a destroyed culture and civilization.

The earliest estimate, like the earliest ad- miration for the rediscovered Gothic art, was based on these superficial forms. For many years Gothic architecture was re- garded, demonstrated and restored solely on the basis of its recorded forms, the centring of its arches, the contours of its mouldings, the nature and design of its or- nament. Commentators on Gothic art pro- duced one silly theory after another, praised inordinately its secondary qualities, and generally dealt with it after a purely em- pirical fashion. Amateur architects and builders copied its details (or satirized them) in wood and plaster, and the re- sults were deplorable. " Strawberry Hill Gothic," " Carpenter's Gothic," " Church- warden Gothic," " Victorian Gothic " (all

effective titles applied by the scoffers) sufficiently express the real quality of this
catastrophic product which bore no earthly
relationship to Gothic itself so far as its
substance is concerned, and only the most
distant resemblance to its forms.

Following the "enlightened amateur"
came the scholar and the archæologist, and
recently the effort has insistently been made
to probe deeper and to determine the nature
and content of the style on a more scientific
basis. The unique and supreme organic
system of Mediæval architecture at its best,
was discovered and analyzed, and this, expressed with great accuracy and after the
most approved "scientific method," was
brought forward as the essence and the cri-
terion of Gothic. According to the pro-
tagonists of this cult "Gothic" architecture
is that alone wherein the groined, ribbed,
pointed vault exists; where this controls the
remainder of the organism, and where all
things develop from, or are made subservi-
ent to, this particular scheme of construction. Conversely it follows, and is so stated,
that any building where vaults of this nature do not exist, or were not contemplated,
cannot be called Gothic. The consequences

are both complicated and (one would suppose) embarrassing. A thirteenth-century cathedral in some town in France is Gothic, but an adjoining dwelling, built at the same time, and perhaps by some of the cathedral workmen, is not. Westminster Abbey is Gothic, but Lincoln and Exeter are not, for the vault system does not logically determine the other details. The choir of Canterbury is Gothic, but a parish church constructed at the same time is not, if it happens to have a wooden roof, or, if vaulted, its pier sections are too large, and its walls are thick enough to take the vault thrusts without flying buttresses.

Of course in a way it is a quarrel over a word. If the world wishes to adopt the name " Gothic " and use it in the narrowly restricted sense indicated above, very well, only some other name must be discovered to describe the great and comprehensive impulse and product of which " Gothic," in that sense, will be only a sub-species. Now this word has been in universal use for five hundred years to indicate not a detail (albeit the most important) of construction, but the whole body of art produced during the preceding five centuries to express the

[xi]

concrete civilization of Catholic Europe. Deliberately to reverse the connotation of the word, giving it an entirely new and very restricted meaning, seems to me illogical, unreasonable and even puerile. It smacks of the meticulous pedantry of nineteenth-century Teutonism and is on a par with the philological testing of religious doctrine, the psychological determination of philosophical postulates, and the solution of the problem of life by the methods of a mechanistic physiological determinism. If the organic system of Gothic construction deserves (as it does) a special nomenclature, let us find or invent the right word, but for the spirit and impulse, the great body of artistic production, and specifically the unique architecture of the Christian Middle Ages, let us retain the venerable word " Gothic," for all the world knows what this indicates, even though it has a nebulous idea of what it means.

Within the space of six lectures it is, of course, quite impossible to do more than indicate some few of the salient points in the system I have tried to establish as the one that must be developed if the architecture of Mediævalism is to be appreciated at its full value. All I have tried to do is to stimulate interest in the great epoch of Christian civilization and to deal, however superficially, with its architectural expression as a supremely organic and living thing. If I have succeeded in the slightest degree, then it is possible for those who wish to follow the subject further to find in many volumes of scholarly and authoritative character the careful working out of the various qualities in Mediævalism I have endeavoured to epitomize. The last decade is notable for the books that have been written along the lines of sympathetic, constructive and stimulating interpretation of the Middle Ages. At the head of the list I should place without question "Mont-Saint-Michel and Chartres," by Henry Adams (Houghton, Mifflin Company), and " The Mediæval Mind," by Henry Osborne Taylor (Macmillan Company). The two books supplement each other and should be read together; so used, profound scholarship and an almost miraculous vision meet together and re-create Mediævalism before our eyes. " The Thirteenth, Greatest of Centuries," by Dr. Walsh (Catholic Summer School Press), is also an authoritative compendium of quite priceless information, while " Reformation and Renaissance," by J. M. Stone (E. P. Dutton & Company), and " The Catholic Church, the Renaissance and Protestantism," by Alfred Baudrillart (Kegan Paul, Trench, Trübner & Co.), deal definitely with the transition from the Middle Ages to modernism. The great introductory essay in Montalembert's " Monks of the West " still remains the authoritative pronouncement on monasticism. Political theory and practice are clearly outlined in " Political Theories of the Middle Ages," by Dr. Otto Gierke (Cambridge University Press), and in " A History of Mediæval Political Theory," by R. W. and A. J. Carlyle (G. P. Putnam's Sons). For a clear and lucid statement of Mediæval philosophy, in concise form, I know no better books than the two first named, by Mr. Adams and Mr. Taylor. Of course the works of St. Thomas Aquinas are now fully translated and St. Bernard is generally available. Unfortunately Hugh of St. Victor still awaits his translator and his commentator. There are many works on the guilds and the industrial and economic organization of the Middle Ages, e.g. " Industrial and Commercial History of England," by Thorold Rogers, " Village Communities in the East and West," by Sir Henry Maine, " The English Village Community," by F. Seebohm, and " English Guilds," published by the Early English Text Society. Two recent books, " The Servile State," by Hilaire Belloc (F. N. Foulis), and " The Real Democracy," by Mann, Sievers and Cox (Longmans, Green & Co.), draw a striking contrast between the Mediæval and modern industrial systems, and as well between the guilds and contemporary trades unionism.

Of the books dealing primarily with architecture I should place first Arthur Kingsley Porter's "Lombard Architecture" (Yale University Press) and his " Mediæval Architecture " (Baker & Taylor Company). Professor Moore's " Gothic Architecture " (Macmillan & Company) is direct, concise and sympathetic, though I must dissent *in toto* from his limitation of the title " Gothic " to the masonry-vaulted structures of France. "A History of Gothic Art in England," by Edward S. Prior (George Bell & Sons), " Gothic Architecture in England " (B. T. Batsford) and

" Introduction to English Church Architecture " (The Oxford University Press), both by Francis Bond, deal admirably with English Gothic; and Professor Lethaby's "Westminster Abbey and the King's Craftsmen " (E. P. Dutton) gives a vivid idea of the methods of building during the Middle Ages.

Cardinal Gasquet has written brilliantly on the later Middle Ages and the beginnings of the Reformation, particularly in his " Henry VIII and the English Monasteries " (John C. Nimmo), " The Eve of the Reformation " (Putnam & Company), and " The Old English Bible and Other Essays " (George Bell & Son). Should there be those who care to read more that I have written along somewhat similar lines, I would suggest " The Ruined Abbeys of Great Britain " (James Pott), " The Gothic Quest " (Doubleday, Page & Company), " The Ministry of Art " (Houghton, Mifflin Company), and " Heart of Europe " (Charles Scribner's Sons).

Finally, for gaining something of the wonderful spirit of Mediævalism at first hand, there remain the epics and verses of the period in their original form, " Morte d'Arthur," by Sir Thomas Mallory, first, of course, with " The High History of the Holy Grail," the latter admirably translated by Sebastian Evans (Dent & Company), and the " Song of Roland." " Romance Vision and Satire " is a collection of translations into modern English by Miss Jessie Weston (Houghton, Mifflin Company) of much of the earliest English verse, including the marvellous " Pearl," which is one of the most beautiful poems in the world. As translations they are far from exact, but the original spirit is marvellously preserved. Probably the best way to get at " Pearl " is to read the Golancz text, with Miss Weston's version as a " crib "; the Golancz translation is quite impossible. Of course in the end Dante remains the great Mediæval synthesis, the " Divine Comedy " standing alone in power and beauty and exaltation — the very Middle Ages made visible.

It is hardly necessary to say that this list is no more exhaustive than it is erudite. I have purposely chosen only those books that are non-technical, easily available, and written in English. Mediævalism is the study of a lifetime, for it is that great cycle of five centuries wherein Christianity created for itself a world as nearly as possible made in its own image, a world that in spite of the wars and the desecrations, the ignorance and the barbarism and the " restorations " of modernism has left us monuments and records and traditions of a power and beauty and nobility without parallel in history. For three years the slow destruction of five centuries has been accelerated to a degree that passes belief, and the ruin of great art is symbolical of the equal ruin that is wrought in the last and lingering vestiges of an almost forgotten Christian civilization. If the wide desolation of war proves but the clearing of the field for the return of the spirit in life, and the mode of life, that once had issue in the Gothic art of a Catholic Europe, the price exacted from the world will not be too great to pay for so glorious a restoration.

RALPH ADAMS CRAM.

WHITEHALL, SUDBURY,
MASSACHUSETTS,
4th August, 1917.

CONTENTS

THE SUBSTANCE OF GOTHIC

The Substance of Gothic

LECTURE I

THE QUARRY OF ANTIQUITY

WE are called upon at this time to re-
estimate our philosophies, to test by newly
revealed criteria those concrete dogmas
and formulæ accepted so generally and for
so long a time as axiomatic: to interpret
anew, and in the light of an impossible
catastrophe, phenomena that had taken their
places in a scheme of things that is for us
no longer definitive or even convincing.
Two years have cleft history in halves, and
once more, as so often in the past, a long
building-up of linked and sequent events
stops suddenly short, cut by a colossal sword.
A new order begins, the nature of which
we cannot definitely determine; a new
order subject to progressive revelation, and
explicit only in one thing, its difference in
every great and every little detail from all
that went before.

These sudden severances are sufficiently familiar to us in the past: so Hellenic civilization was cut short that Rome might have her day: so Rome fell and Mediterranean culture yielded to the barbarism of the North: so again this, when it had made of itself the high expression of Christianity, gave way in its turn to a new thing, the consistent, logical, and well-rounded episode we have called Modern Civilization, working out its destiny through the three phases of Renaissance, Reformation, and Revolution that it might achieve at last its fruition through intellectualism, secularism, and materialism, and in its turn break down and disappear, to give place to that new era the nature of which is still in the balance, while a world in arms hammers out its unknown future on bloody anvils and in the shadow of unimaginable conflict.

For us, looking backward over the clearly defined perspective of the past, it is easy to trace the great clefts in history as they cut like giant crevasses the rolling plateau of life, but when a bottomless chasm suddenly splits itself through the midst of our own normal existence, without warning and in violation of all personal experience, it is as though on some summer morning the field at the bottom of the garden disappeared, with a crash of rending worlds, in an unfathomable pit, raw and horrible, that rent itself with the speed of lightning through well-known meadows and hills and forests, leaving on the one side the shaken garden on the black edge of catastrophe, on the other all the once familiar world of cities and of men, no longer approachable, no longer even assured in its existence.

The war the whole world said could never come, but the war that came nevertheless, to the confusion of human assurance, means many things, most of which are still unrevealed, but two are sufficiently clear and they are, first: that the world after the war will be, for good or ill, an entirely new world; and second: that every preconceived idea of the man of the nineteenth century must now submit itself to the process of re-estimation. All that was essentially of the last epoch, i.e. from 1414 to 1914, in religion, philosophy, and the conduct of life, must subject itself to a new testing, for the blast of war is purging away the dross, and the alchemy of a world's agony is transmuting base metal into refined gold. Once more we are driven back from a world of phenomena to the everlasting verities. If by the grace of God (and our own humility) we are able to lay hold of them, we have won for ourselves a new Middle Ages, a new Renaissance; and what now seems the peril of a new Dark Ages passes away.

In its essential contributions to religion, philosophy, and the conduct of life the last era of five centuries was, I believe, proceeding on lines that were in general malefic rather than beneficent, for it failed ignobly in the chief object of life, which is the development of character. Its contributions to material wealth, to intellectual competence, to mastery of the forces of nature, to ease, luxury, manners, to physical well-being and scientific achievement, were unexampled in their magnitude, but in the concrete appreciation of these things (in themselves so full of potency), the failure was almost complete, and in the end the breakdown of character has been ominous and significant. It is true, however, that the by-products of the process were often of great value and these may in time be made operative to admirable ends.

In its estimate of the past, its interpretation of history, the conclusions were as erroneous as the method was ill-judged, and the result was an entirely false standard of comparative values and an almost complete negativing of the constructive powers for good inherent in the recorded annals of human experience and adventure. Finally it was an age that was responsible for the breakdown and almost complete disappearance of art as a vital force in society, a condition that, we must always remember, is unique in history. However low an art, or all the arts, may have fallen at certain rhythmical intervals in the past, there was always an irreducible minimum left, a nucleus which, as culture returned and civilization began again, served as the little leaven that in the end lightened the whole lump and made possible once more a new epoch of artistic achievement.

I wish to speak to you during this course of lectures of one of the greatest of all the arts as it ran its course from the time of its recovery in the west under Charlemagne to its transformation at the time of the Renaissance, the last episode occurring in England at the end of the reign of Henry

[5]

VIII — a period of seven centuries which exactly covers the era of specifically Christian civilization in Europe. I wish to do this partly because architecture is the most human and general of all the arts and one which exerts its beneficent influence most widely; partly because it was the first of the arts to break down and disappear in the nineteenth century, maintaining itself since then only as a wistful and yet ardent effort at premeditated recovery; partly because the nineteenth century efforts at a critical and philosophical estimate of this particularly significant era of architecture seem to me peculiarly disastrous, in that they have resulted either in very erroneous conclusions as to the art itself and its position relative to the other phases of the same art, or in a method of estimate that eliminated all the inner and essential qualities that gave the architecture of this time its unique claim on a lasting admiration, and its peculiar significance for us of this day and generation.

Two things may happen to art: transformation in form and transformation in content. The first is a more or less regular process operating, as does all human development, physical, mental, and spiritual, not by steady progression, or by spiral ascension, as was once pleasantly feigned by the evolutionists of the nineteenth century, but by sudden and almost instantaneous leaps both forward and backward, with long following periods either of slow progression or of equally slow degeneration. " Catastrophic " is a word that may be used in opposition to the old and no longer credible " evolutionary," to express the sudden and even violent changes in direction and variations in impulsive force that, acting in obedience to a mysterious stimulus, the source of which science cannot determine, initiate those changes in species and those rhythmical eras in progress and retrogression that determine human life while they baffle all mechanistic systems of thought and become the nemesis of " the scientific method." These violent actions and reactions are very evident in all the arts and they determine those stylistic changes that give it so much of its intense vitality and make it so exactly an expression of life itself. Such was the revolution effected in fifty years when the Romanesque of the Normans gave place to the Gothic of the Franks, or that

[7]

other of an equal period of time, though varying in date as between one race and another, whereby Mediæval art became the art of the Renaissance. Transformation in content is a different thing altogether: it cannot be called periodic for it has happened only once, and that so recently that the event is almost within our own memory.

However great the transformations in form that have occurred from time to time in the past, they have never altered the content of art itself, which has always remained a perfectly definite thing, an inalienable heritage of man, working within certain clearly circumscribed lines, in accordance with an unchanging method, toward an unvarying end. It has presupposed the existence of beauty, relative at first but absolute in fact, and susceptible always, in its absolute form, of approximation and, though rarely, of achievement. This beauty — of form, line, colour, chiaroscuro, tone, melody, harmony, rhythm — has been desirable in itself, and because of its power of sensuous delight, but even more as a means of expressing symbolically, and therefore sacramentally, those spiritual adventures, experiences, and achievements which transcend the sphere of the physical and the intellectual, and therefore can be expressed only after a symbolical or sacramental fashion. In other words beauty, which is the vehicle of art, may be, and has been, used for the expression for man, and from one to another, of those highest things of life and experience, which are, by their very nature, unsusceptible of other manifestation.

Now this beauty is not, either as beauty or as a mode of expression, a matter of personal idiosyncrasy. Specific individuals, sometimes called artists, precipitate it, give it form, infuse it with an element of their own personality, and shape it in the concrete through power of craftsmanship, in them more highly developed than amongst their fellows. This does not make the art their own: the beauty with which they deal is not the emanation of their own idiosyncrasies, it is as universal and immutable as right and wrong or the law of gravitation. The artist has a certain sensitiveness to beauty just as others are sensitive to philosophical, mathematical, or mechanical stimuli, therefore he can isolate this beauty better than another. The artist is

a trained, exquisite, and competent craftsman in stone, wood, marble, pigments,
musical notes, what you will; working with
ardour and devotion in accordance with the
slowly developed laws of his particular
craft, therefore able to do what others cannot do. The artist contributes an element
of his own personality, so bringing his art
down to earth, making it human, and vitalizing it with personality; giving it distinc-
tion, in other words. Yet all this does not
make the art his own, for unless there is behind him a communal self-consciousness,
unless the air is quick with impulses and
desires of the whole people eager for the
expression of their own spiritual experiences and emotions, or at the least for the
visible manifestation of that beauty in which
they themselves can find pleasure and content, then the art of the individual, however great he may be, is a fond thing, vainly
imagined, and no part of any life save only
his own. Until the last hundred years, or
even less, the artist was a mouthpiece and a
servant, though increasingly laggard in his
service. He is now a rebel and an outlaw,
and though he himself may be a greater
artist than his forebears, his place in society

is fundamentally different. Under these conditions he cannot prolong the succession, and becomes the last of his race.

This change from universal art to peculiar art has actually taken place within the century, and transformation in content has been effected, for the first time in history. Within twenty years the inevitable result has shown itself, and the personal, idiosyncratic art which, through a number of very great geniuses at the end of the last century, deceived us by its competence into the belief that art had been born again (or was still continuing) has passed, and we are now confronted by certain anomalous products, in all the arts, which are not art at all but the mouthings of anarchy, the pathological reactions of a spiritual degeneration now in the last stages of its progress.

It is significant that this phenomenon should synchronize exactly with the revealing breakdown of what is known as modern civilization. This civilization proceeded to its supreme achievement through four centuries of cumulative development and ever accelerating momentum, cresting at last in the second decade of the twentieth century only to break as a wave breaks, and fall in destroying dissolution. During the same period the fate of art was being accomplished and it is now involved in the same ruin. That this is not a final estate we must all be persuaded. Nothing exactly like it has ever happened before, it is true, but nothing even remotely like modern civilization has ever happened before. From time to time under the racking shock of disappointment, disillusionment, and vanity wounded to death; under the staggering horrors of the piling of a Pelion of human agony on the Ossa of human infamy, we doubt if this is not indeed the end of the world, the preliminary skirmish of Armageddon. For those at least who hold to their faith in Christianity this natural fear breaks down under a resurgent faith and they are able to look beyond catastrophe to a consequent regeneration, so believing that once more the sane sequence of life will be re-established after the great readjustment has been accomplished.

This readjustment, which will affect every category of life, involves a new scrutiny of all the things man has done in the past and a new estimating of the motive forces behind these actions. In the red light of war, the last era of human activity, the " Modern Era " shows itself in many ways as a "sport," a development along lines not implied by the pre-Renaissance world but striking off at an unexpected and not wholly advantageous angle. It is now confronted by the blunt " No Thorough-fare " of an annihilating war, and of necessity there must be a certain measure of return toward the point where the wrong path was chosen. In the abnormal development of the peculiar elements of modern civilization several essential matters, essential to sane and righteous life, have been lost sight of, and their determination and recovery form the first task of the world that follows the War. Immediately, therefore, we must expect, and ensure, a new scrutinizing of history, largely for the purpose of discerning just what the vital impulses were that lay behind those epochs of civilization more successful than our own, in order that these may be made operative again toward that great regeneration that must follow war, if we are not to sink back into a period of Dark Ages differing only from those that followed the fall of Rome in the greater blackness of their shame and the increased profundity of their oblivion.

This is my excuse for taking up with you the question of the historical development of one of the arts, and at a time when all of us have little heart for the amenities of life. But art is *not* an amenity of life: that is just the point. Modern civilization has made it that, and in this also modern civilization is wrong. It is an integral part of life itself, as indispensable as religion or ethics or philosophy. It is the heritage of all, not the appanage of the few, though it has become the latter through the operation of the false principles inherent in our scheme of existence. For more than four centuries the process of degeneration has been working itself out, though it was only during the nineteenth century that each of the arts finally succumbed, architecture going first, music and poetry coming last. But for the War the case would have appeared hopeless and we could have confronted nothing but a life from which art in all its forms was definitely excluded. Now the War gives us not only a new hope, but a new impulse; a hope that art in all its myriad forms may come again, an impulse to go back and learn more, and along different lines, of the art of the past and of what made it what it was, in order that we may contribute something along these lines to the new civilization that must arduously be built up on the ruins of a great failure.

Art, in its many forms, is the most reliable history of a time, largely because it does *not* deal with concrete facts which, so far as absolute and final truth is concerned, are of the nature of statistics, proverbially said to be of the third and highest degree of lies. The modern historical method deals with facts, which are further emphasized in their error by the application of a mechanistic psychology, and the result is about as illuminating as is the method of the "higher criticism" when applied to the Scriptures, or that of Morelli in the case of attributions in painting. If you would know what sort of men and women they were who lived at any time, — how they thought and felt, and why, — and if you would approach some sound critical estimate of the life they made, the world of thought and feeling in which they lived, go back to their art; to their architecture, painting, and sculpture, their poetry, drama, and music, their industrial arts, their liturgics, and their ceremonial. To create a fabulous epoch out of chronicles, dates, concrete acts, and documents, all fused in the alembic of a personal and arbitrary psychology, and then to test the art of that epoch by this curious philtre, is folly: far more sensible is it to interpret and co-ordinate these same events in the light of the art that is in itself the clear and naïve revelation of the soul of any time.

Behind our own era, which as I have said begins with the first stirrings of the Renaissance, lies the epoch of the Middle Ages. For four hundred years it was misjudged and misrepresented by historians and forgotten by the world at large. Three quarters of a century ago it was rediscovered, and the romanticism of the early nineteenth century in France and England, the Catholic revival in religion, the Gothic restoration in architecture were its first visible manifestations. Naturally they were all more or less tinged by superficiality, by a pale copying of externals, and naturally also they synchronized with the triumphant achievements of that modern civilization against which they were a protest. For both reasons the first movement broke down, and the elapsed years of the twentieth century saw its submergence under an universally victorious modernism. Now this victory shows itself as no other than ignominious defeat, and war sweeps the field clear for new things. Can we, therefore, attempt a new method, and as the echoes of annihilation die away over the wide ruin of a dead era, try once more to get nearer the secret of this great epoch of Christian civilization and recover something of its potency for ourselves?

Much of what we need now, and shall need increasingly when rebuilding takes the place of destruction, lies there, — more than we suspect, or, for the moment, should welcome. Confining ourselves, therefore, to the single art of architecture, let us see if we can discover what this paramount art of the Middle Ages really was, what it grew from, and by the operation of what forces, — what it has for us today, not only in the re-creation and rehabilitation of our own dead art of architecture, but what it can show us of the methods and accomplishment of a great and very sane era of culture and civilization.

When, fat with her wealth, her power, and her pride of life, Rome fell before the barbarian invaders, the destinies of Europe were changed forever. The Mediterranean races gave place to those from the Baltic, the south yielded to the north, civil power to ecclesiastical, secular Christianity to monastic, patristic theology to the personal religion of the people; pagan and Alexandrian philosophy was for the time extinguished, and nationalism was merged in tribalism. An "act of oblivion" was passed by the dominant and savage north; for three centuries progressive forgetfulness held dominion while a new race of men hammered out the rough foundations of a new world and the shaking successors of St. Peter sat in a desolated Rome, the only centre of approximate order in a whirlpool of anarchy.

It is as hard to comprehend the complete extinguishing of classical civilization in the fifth century, as it would be for us today to imagine the total obliteration of all the achievements of the last four centuries, yet the real and the supposititious cases are the same, and what has once happened may happen again. In hardly more than an hundred years a State coterminous with the world, proud, wealthy, invincible in the field, boasting a superficial culture, insolent in its assurance, magnificent in all its outward forms of art and pageantry, broke down, crumbled and utterly disappeared. Rome declared her ability to extend her own culture, with her civil and military dominion, to all the barbarous peoples of three continents, and in the end found that, instead, she had sunk to the level of those she would succour, who, themselves the victors, entered in and took possession. From all sides, east, west, north, south, savage hordes crept over the marble villas and pleasant gardens and fertile farms of Britain, Gaul, the Rhineland, Africa, Syria, leaving only ruin and desolation. Crept on the great summer resorts with their terraced palaces and their luxurious and profligate life, the resorts that made the mountain valleys and delicate rivers and Mediterranean headlands and beaches pleasure haunts of infinite delight. One by one they vanished in flame and sack, until the forests returned, the sand washed higher, obliterating even the calcined fragments of an architecture such as the world had never seen before. Alaric, Genseric, Attila, Ricimer, one hardy and scornful leader after another, laid siege to Rome, captured and sacked it, and returned with booty that weighed down the thousands of horses and the tens of thousands of warriors. At last the wolves prowled unmolested amongst the temples and basilicas, the baths and fora and palaces, of what had once been Imperial Rome, while pestilence and famine decimated all Italy, and deep woods and poisonous marshes took the place of crowded cities and broad acres of farms and gardens.

Even memory of what had been was lost, at least for the west. On the Bosporus a New Rome preserved a lingering tradition that died away before a subtle and encroaching Orientalism and a degenerate but delectable Hellenism. In the Benedictine monasteries, now fast rising as fortresses of refuge in the midst of catastrophe, manuscripts from devastated libraries were gathered together and preserved, but the spirit that alone possessed any element of vitality was now anti-pagan and ascetic, and the monks only guarded what they would not use. And as the last memory of a classical past had disappeared, so for several centuries the new power — northern, Christian and monastic — showed no signs of creating anything to take its place. Culture, even of the most rudimentary kind, was non-existent: there was no art of any sort, neither architecture, painting, sculpture, poetry, music, drama, nor even the minor arts of the craftsman. Education was practically unknown, save the bare rudiments that the priest must have, and of learning there was no vestige in all Europe.

It was a good clean blood, however, that had entered the veins of Europe in place of the poisoned and vitiated blood of the south, and health conquered disease. Clovis, who had defeated the degenerate Romans at the Battle of Soissons in 486 and accepted Christianity ten years later, had established a new State in Gaul, Catholic, in opposition to the Arian heresies of the other converted northern tribes. St. Benedict in the year 529 had founded his Order that was to act as the spiritual stimulus of Europe for a thousand years. In 587 Spain had been won over from Arianism to Catholicism, in 590 St. Gregory became Pope and wrenched the Church from the mire of the great degeneration, and in 597 sent St. Augustine to begin the work of regeneration in England. It was a good beginning, but the power of dissolution was greater than that of recovery; outside the monasteries culture and decency disappeared, Mohammedanism rushed in like a flood against the narrowing frontiers of Christianity, Spain was lost and the future seemed to hold nothing but ruin and an ending of all things.

With the year 732 the real recovery began, for it was then, at the Battle of Tours, that Charles Martel — the Hammer that not only smote back the Mohammedan invasion but forged the mighty fabric of the House of the Carolings — halted the Moors in their invasion of Europe that already had swept nearly to the gates of Paris. Thirty-five years later Charlemagne began the rebuilding of European civilization, crushing the degenerate Lombards in Italy, and the savage Saxons and Bavarians; destroying the Avars in Austria, winning back northern Spain, and giving a measure of unity to a distracted and dislocated Europe.

It is the fashion to attribute to Charlemagne himself the credit for the sudden if

short recovery of art and learning and culture of the last half of the eighth century,
but as a matter of fact they and he were
linked results of the same slow process of
regeneration that began with St. Benedict
in his cave at Subiaco. He was of course
the visible agency of the culminating
achievement, for God always works through
individual men and women in the development of His Will as this is exhibited on
earth, and it is only just that for all time
the first fruits of Christian society, organized and operative, should bear his name.

We must realize, however, that already a
great process of development had begun,
the end of which was to be a definitely
Christian system of life, when every phase
of thought and action should be interpenetrated by a specifically Catholic force. The
entire space of time from Theodoric to
Otho the Great, exactly five centuries, is
given over to the struggles of a new spirit
to achieve the mastery, with its partial success under Charlemagne, which was immediately followed by complete failure, as
this in its turn was succeeded by a more
vigorous effort that was quickly crowned
by success.

There is something almost mysterious in the way in which the idea of secular world-Empire grew under the Cæsars, simultaneously with the idea of a world-Church. This is the great contest of the first five centuries of the Christian era, determined at last against the imperial State, but not as yet in favour of the imperial Church. As Gregorovius says, the Empire stood for slavery and despotism, with complete poverty in creative ideas in civilization. All that tended to raise the intellectual spirit to the higher regions of thought was either non-existent, or acclimatized from other lands. On the other hand, the idea of the spiritual world-State was developing simultaneously, and Rome, the Eternal City, no sooner lost all claim to the title, as a material force, than she was taken over by the new spiritual force, regenerated, made again of universal dominion, and her claim to the epithet " Eternal " vindicated anew. When the Empire fell the Church was already an universal organization under the supreme direction of the Bishop of Rome who was acknowledged to be the Vicar of God on Earth, and the imperium passed to her, of right, though the process of transfer took some time to accomplish — the epoch known in history as the Dark Ages.

After their first successful invasions, the Goths maintained a remote civil dominion for Rome, or rather for the old Imperial Roman idea, but after their defeat by the emissaries of Byzantium, the last vestiges of secular supremacy died away and its impotent traditions maintained only a pale continuance at Ravenna. It is during this time that the Church made herself the dominant influence in Europe, first by the conversion of the Lombards and the other heretical tribes, second by her successful warfare against the Idea of the East as this was embodied in the exarchs. Through the first she exterminated the Arian and other heresies, united Christianity and made it Catholic over all Europe. Through the second she beat back the peril of governmental absolutism and made possible the Christian social system, which was feudalism.

During the great warfare that achieved such vast victories there was little possibility of a creative culture that would have expression in the form of art of any kind; the issues were too colossal, the crises too acute. Not until the time of Charlemagne could society begin to reap the benefits of its great enfranchisement, but then the ground had been won and held, though insecurely, and the artistic results inevitably followed.

What these results were, in architectural form, I shall try to show in my next lecture; in the meantime I wish to place before you the material from which these results were obtained.

Neither architecture, nor any other art, is the product of individual genius. There is no such thing, properly speaking, as a "new" style, and there never can be a "new" art cut off from the succession of the past. Perhaps this is why the supposititious art of today — *art nouveau,* cubist, impressionist, imagist, what you will — is not art at all, but an unpleasant fiction of auto-suggestion. The art of the Carolingian era was genuine art, as far as it went, and it was based on certain remains of the antecedent epoch and worked out largely by means of enduring principles and traditions inherited from the same time. The strictly pagan remains of Rome, southern France, Trèves were completely ignored, though in the eighth century they were ten times as numerous as now. Instead recourse was had to pagan architecture as it had been adapted by Christianity, and of this there was also far more than has been preserved to our own time.

This "Early Christian Architecture" had its habitat in four widely severed places, but all of them available to Europe through merchants, travellers, and pilgrims going to or sent from these then flourishing centres. Rome, Ravenna, Constantinople, and Syria were, in varying degrees, centres of wealth and activity in the Dark Ages, and even then intercourse amongst them was constant, and of a magnitude we can hardly appreciate. In Rome were the great Constantinian basilicas, — St. Peter's, St. John Lateran, Sta. Maria Maggiore, San Clemente, Sta. Agnese, and scores of others of lesser magnitude, all couched in much the same style, all magnificent, and touched with the mysterious splendour of the recognized centre of spiritual authority and of civil dominion. Always simple in plan, though varying considerably in design (some being of the most archaic basilican type, others with lofty galleries over the aisles, long ranges of

clerestory windows, and added accessories
of chapels and baptisteries), they all were
rich with antique columns of precious
marbles, sheathing of porphyry and ala-
baster, golden and azure mosaics, and altars
and ambos and thrones of the most sumptuous design and the most rare materials. To
them men turned naturally first of all, and
then to Constantinople, where Justinian had
but recently immortalized himself as the
most princely builder of all time, through
his sequence of great domed temples, as
incredible in their magnificence as they
were masterly in their original scheme of
construction. Hagia Sophia was of course
the everlasting wonder of all Christendom,
but there were countless other smaller
churches, such as St. Irene and Holy Apostles, and in Salonika, Trebizond, Bethle-
hem, Jerusalem, as well. Numbers of these
have wholly disappeared under Turkish
conquest, and we can only guess at their
nature, but there were many in the eighth
century, well known to the people of the
time, of which we know only by contemporary records.

In Syria, which is now for us only a barren desert, there were the great cities of a

THE QUARRY OF ANTIQUITY

once sumptuous civilization, and it is here, half hidden under sand and debris, that much has recently been found by Professor Butler of Princeton that gives another aspect to Christian archæology. Here were three great schools of architecture, counting from north to south, which seem to contain more of the elements of Mediæval art than are to be found elsewhere. It is from Syria, apparently, that Diocletian drew the builders of his amazing palace at Spalato, and that Justinian found those who were to develop for him the magnificent building of his reign. In the south were the curious structures, wholly of stone, that de Vogüe has so carefully studied, with their piers instead of columns, their close-set transverse nave and aisle arches carrying roofs of stone slabs, and their arch abutments precisely like those we find centuries later at Sant' Ambrogio, Milan. Here also we find, as at Zor-ah, the primitive domical churches, polygonal in plan, set within a square, and with absidioles in the angles, that are the prototypes of San Vitale and Aix-la-Chapelle. In the middle school, the closely built piers of the south give place to very wide spacing, with broad round arches and low clerestories of narrow windows. The aisles are vaulted in stone, the roofs are of wood. Here also we discover the norm of the great flanking towers of the west ends of Norman and Gothic abbeys and cathedrals, though at first they are low and rise but little above the roof levels. The complete parallel that exists between the exterior architectural treatment of these churches and that of the twelfth century Romanesque work of southern France, is startling. Columns are used on the apses and chapels precisely as they are employed there, and with the arched corbel table form the prototype of the pilaster strips and cornices of Lombardy and the Rhine. In the north columns, once more, are generally used as supports; there are three apses, instead of one, and these, curiously enough, are often square in plan, even the main sanctuary, like the early British church that fixed the permanent type of square-ended plan in England. Another singular innovation is the lifting of the side chapels into towers of several stories framing in the apse; a device which appears later at Como and goes thence to the Rhineland, where it becomes a characteristic and entirely local feature. In this northern school the feeling is predominantly Greek, in form as well as in decoration. The carved ornament is crisp and clean, and merges rapidly into the intricate and brilliant patterning of Byzantine art.

Finally, we have Ravenna with its work of Theodoric and the Byzantine exarchs; the tomb of Galla Placidia, San Vitale, the two churches of Sant' Apollinare, the baptistery, and probably other monuments now destroyed. Both plan types are here, basilican and domical, together with the little tomb church, which is cruciform, with a rudimentary central tower. Less magisterial than the Roman basilicas, less magnificent than the gold and marble wonders of Byzantium, the work is more akin to the temper of the north and west, and more adaptable because of its scale. Such a plan as that of San Vitale would stimulate any builder to creative action, as it did; and the old school of craftsmen seemed to last longer here than anywhere else, except perhaps amongst the Comacini. At Pomposa and Bagnacavallo, near by, and at Grado and Parenzo in Istria, are other examples of Ravennesque work; and altogether the city of the exarchs and of the great northern barbarian, Theodoric, who proved himself so sane and beneficent a ruler, offered in the eighth century a series of models that could only serve as a strong incentive the moment a real, if transient, vitality appeared in society itself.

LECTURE II

THE AGE OF CHARLEMAGNE

WITH the destruction of the magnificent governmental system of Rome, all semblance of civil order and authority was lost. Sense of nationality was non-existent as yet, racial lines had not asserted themselves, and by a perfectly natural process the feudal system grew up around the strong men, and with the cordial approval of the Church. In principle, and even more in its working out, it proved a most admirable and efficient scheme of political and social organization. From an economic standpoint it was more successful and far more just and beneficent than the industrial slavery that preceded it, or the capitalistic régime that has taken its place. This was particularly true after it had fully developed the guild system which, during the golden era of the central Middle Ages, guaranteed freedom, justice, and honourable status for industry of every kind.

Politically the results were equally good. Every man owed service and a certain amount of tribute in kind to the over-lord next above him, who in his turn owed similar service and truage, with the others of his class, to the baron or count or bishop or abbot in the next rank of the hierarchy, and so on up to the sovereign authority over the tribe or race or other governmental unit. On his own part the over-lord was in theory bound to defend the life and land of his vassals and to see that justice was done amongst them. The result was that from the unit of the family up through the commune, the county, the kingdom, and — from Charlemagne on, as a general thing — the Empire, every man was an integral part of a small, manageable and personal group, not as now, a negligible point in a vast and abstract proposition where all personal relationship, personal duty, personal obligation are impossible.

Out of this orderly organization grew the sense of honour, and of faithful personal service on the one hand, of generosity and protection on the other, and we can understand nothing of Mediævalism unless we give just regard to this almost fundamental element in its constitution. Of course I am stating here only an ideal, for there were innumerable cases of failure, on the one side or the other, to live up to this ideal; cases of rebellion and treachery; of oppression, cruelty, and dishonour, but there is good evidence to show that the ideal was then as nearly approached in the majority of instances, as, we will say, the ideals of democracy have been approached in the nineteenth and twentieth centuries.

I am sensible of the fact that some of you may be very much shocked at hearing me praise feudalism, and call it, as I most certainly do, the nearest recorded approach to the Christian commonwealth. If you indeed are stirred by this sentiment then that is what I mean when I refer to the misinterpretation of history that was one of the salient characteristics of the nineteenth century. The number of things that are called "Mediæval," particularly by political orators, educational experts, and other imperfectly educated people, is astounding. It is a general term of modern, — as "Gothic" was a general term of Renaissance, — contempt, and it is employed with indifferent discretion. Absolutism in government, religious persecution, the Inquisition, untidiness, conservatism, are all cheerfully denominated "Mediæval," in calm disregard of the fact that they are all inventions or practices of the Renaissance, or even, some of them, of more modern times. In the same way, feudalism, which certainly was Mediæval, is used as a synonym for all that is dark, barbarous and oppressive.

A word of warning should be given those who, very properly, turn to available contemporary documents, particularly those of a legal nature, to obtain a first-hand idea of feudalism as an actuality. The legal theories of feudalism were very lightly regarded in actual practice, for there it was never a question of what the law was, or might be made, but what had been established by ancient custom and universal acceptance. The insanity of law-making and law-tinkering which has been and is the curse of modern society is hardly three centuries old and was then unknown. Government is not now a system of laws but of decrees, differing little in motive from the irresponsible edicts of absolutism, and the result is general contempt and a flagrant willingness to evade the provisions of these decrees by every possible means. Then the full force of universal custom was supreme; laws were this custom proved and codified, and as a result Law had a force that made it almost imprescriptible, while it represented not fluctuant opinion but the matured results of the interplay of influences both high and low.

A case in point is the shocking " droit de seigneur," so often referred to by superficial students of Mediævalism. There is actually no evidence to prove that this was a recognized custom or even anything but the most sporadic offence, no more representative of feudalism than the alleged " blue laws " are representative of democracy. In the Middle Ages all relationship was personal and direct, and of course much depended on the personality of the overlord, but higher than he was Custom, the unwritten and immemorial law of society; and this custom was far less easily flouted or evaded than are modern laws that are too well known in the methods of their inception and their enforcement to command respect or ensure their obedient acceptance by those who would evade their provisions.

I dare say the later feudalism, as it appeared in the last days of the Middle Ages in Germany, and in other parts of Europe in the earlier Renaissance, was dark, barbarous, and oppressive, but I am speaking of it as it was in the eleventh, twelfth, and thirteenth centuries, while it was the basis of Christian society, and then it certainly was quite the reverse. It came nearer a real democracy than any other of the manifold and optimistic experiments of man, for it more nearly abolished privilege, established equal opportunity and utilized ability, while it fixed the means of production in the hands of the people, guaranteed a fairly even distribution of wealth, organized workmen and craftsmen and artists on a just and equable basis of labour and compensation, and therefore helped in the greatest production of vigorous, righteous, and noble character that is of record in human annals.

As economic feudalism had its flowering in the guild system, so social feudalism grew through the Crusades into the institution of chivalry which, until it degenerated into the licentious pageantry of the Renaissance, was a vital force in society no substitute for which has as yet been found. Of this, however, there was nothing at the moment when

Charlemagne took on himself the co-ordination of the wandering efforts that had preceded him, and the application of them toward the organization of a new State and the development of a new culture. Feudalism was then in its most primitive estate, nothing more than the offensive-defensive alliance of groups of harried and poverty-stricken men for the sheer preservation of life and such poor property as they had.

The monastic system, as it had been organized by St. Benedict, he possessed in an highly developed form, and he used it for its full value. Indeed, without it he could have done nothing, he could hardly have existed, and it is not too much to say that but for the monks from the sixth to the fourteenth century, there would have been no Mediævalism, nor even any civilization at all, and we still might be painting ourselves a dead blue, with woad, as did our ancestors in early Britain.

The Church of the first five centuries had been essentially episcopal, that is, the development and fixing of doctrine, discipline, and ceremonial, the suppression of innumerable heresies, the direction of the conscience both of individuals and of the

Church itself, had been the work of the episcopal order — bishops, metropolitans, patriarchs, with, for at least three of those centuries, the Pope sitting above all and acting as the co-ordinating force. The Church of the two succeeding epochs of five centuries each, was essentially monastic, with the Pope, secure and alone in his supremacy, undisputed spiritual lord of all Christendom, save only the patriarchate of the east which was steadily declining in culture, in moral force, and in civil authority. From the year 529 the monasteries of St. Benedict formed an ever-increasing number of refuges from a world crumbling about men's ears, the only centres of order, of culture (such as it was), of ethical integrity. They rapidly took over many of the functions of the destroyed civil government — education, mercy, the direction of agriculture and industry, the fostering of art and letters — and in that long interval between the destruction of the Roman imperium and the rebirth of sense of nationality served as the centres around which distracted men gathered into communities for self-preservation. If we are tempted at times to disapprove the apparent secularization of abbots, monks, and monasteries, in the Dark Ages and during Mediævalism, we must remember that tasks and duties rightly belonging to the civil order had been taken over by them simply because there was nothing else that would or could administer them, and that therefore they were forced to play a dual rôle if society was to be preserved from total destruction.

The same is true also of the Papacy and the whole Catholic Church. The division of the Empire, the transference of the seat of authority to Constantinople, the abandonment of Europe, and the incursions of the barbarians had left the Pope as the only visible sign of authority, not only in Italy but in all western Europe. Willingly or unwillingly he found himself compelled to exercise on his own part the double function of spiritual head of Christendom and the centre of secular authority. Whether the succeeding pontiffs acquitted themselves well of their enormous task, or ill, is not the question: some did, some did not, but in any case they played a part there was no one else to play, and they were the chief agents in bringing some semblance of order out of chaos, largely through the Benedictine monks who were ready at hand in almost every land, the more barbarous and insecure the better, so far as their own inclinations were concerned.

Apart from the universal conviction throughout Christian Europe, of the unity of the Church, an unity made visible through the identity of doctrine, discipline, and worship between Rome itself and the smallest missions on the far fringes of Christendom, the destruction of sense of nationality and the multitude of feudal groups made Rome still more the one possible centre of union. This enforced secular supremacy may possibly have been unfortunate for the Church in her spiritual aspect, but the fact remains that for a thousand years she was the one fixed and invariable fact in Europe, the one authority that remained unaffected by the rise and fall of kings, of dynasties, of the Empire itself. Heresy could not shake her, schism could not diminish her power. Bad bishops, recreant priests and monks, evil intruders even on the chair of Peter, antipopes in armed contention, all left her in the end just as she had been before, and however hopeless her case from time to

time, reform succeeded in the end, and great
figures like Gregory the Great, Gregory
VII, Innocent III appeared to raise her still
higher than before in power and in visible
glory. Whether we like it or not, the Catholic Church remains the greatest single fact
in human history. It is therefore hardly
to be wondered at that for this same thousand years the Catholic Church should have
seemed to all Christians, and should actually have been, a greater force in secular,
as well as in spiritual affairs, than kings and
emperors.

Now it was during this very period that
culture, civilization, and the arts were born
again, and chiefly that art of architecture
we are considering, since it is the most
brilliant instance of logical and consistent
growth that is of record in the annals of
man, reaching as it did, in the end, a supreme height that staggers the imagination.
It fell with the power that had created it,
for the last five centuries have been of a
temper as different from the " Great Thousand Years " as these were different from
paganism itself. From then on diversity in
religion took the place of unity, the long
contest between Church and State was de-

termined in favour of the secular power, and religion has become less and less a matter of moment. The Catholic Church has now taken its place in general estimation as only the largest amongst some one hundred and forty divisions of Christianity, without material effect in some nations, dominant in the Mediæval sense in none. Nationality has split Europe into self-conscious and mutually inimical fragments as the Reformation split Christianity; and of necessity therefore, the art, and very particularly, the architecture, of the post-Reformation era has been in a category by itself.

In dealing then with the development of architecture from Charlemagne to Henry VIII we must first visualize for ourselves the Europe of that era, though admittedly the task is no easy one. It was in every great and every little respect utterly different to what it is today, while it is cut off from us by five centuries of an entirely new civilization of which we are children by inheritance and therefore almost incapable of thinking back into a time with which we have little sympathy either by temper or by tendency. Summarized, the points to be borne in mind are these. Total extinction of classical civilization, with at first the wiping out even of the memory thereof. A new race taking over the entire direction of affairs, of the north, northern: savage, illiterate, but clean in blood, inordinately vigorous, fresh from the cold hard shores of the Baltic. The extinction of civil government, order, law: the substitution of tribal instincts for those of nationality, and the rapid development of a feudal system of personal relationships, as much in advance of what it superseded as it differed therefrom. Wide extension of Christianity of explicitly Catholic type, with the suppression and extermination of Arianism and all other heresies. Unity of theological belief and religious practices, with the Papacy as the only recognized centre of spiritual authority and as the one indestructible institution in the world. A monastic system, Benedictine by rule, that was rapidly extending itself, through its innumerable monasteries and its equally innumerable missionaries, not only in Christian Europe, but into every neighbouring heathen land as well, and coming in close touch with almost every man, woman, and child as reli-

gious director, educator, civilizer, and unifying power. Such was Europe, if we use
the term geographically; culturally, nation-
ally, Europe was non-existent. Manners,
morals, customs, all had fallen to the lowest
point recorded in history; and learning,
culture, and even decency had fled to the
east, taking refuge with the Mohammedan
Arabs in the Caliphate of Baghdad. Cor-
rupt as the Papacy had become in the general corruption it was all there was of order
in the west, and, vastly strengthened by
a definite accession of temporal power
through the conferring on Pope Stephen by
King Pepin of the Exarchate of Ravenna
in 756, it could at least act as a general
unifying influence both spiritually and
temporally.

Against this single authority Charlemagne first set a new civil power, not in
opposition but in union, and with a breadth
of vision, a practicality of action, that shine
singly in the long night of the Dark Ages.
With a strong hand he reformed the
Church, founded new monasteries, built up
schools, fostered agriculture, and surrounded himself with all the scholars and
artists and craftsmen he could gather from

the four quarters of Europe: Alcuin of Britain, Peter of Pisa, Paul the Doctor, Theodaulphus of Spain, Eberhard, Hincmar, Erugena, Radbertus Maurus.

Charlemagne was not a sudden figure of light and power, shot headlong, cometwise, through the night of the Dark Ages: he was rather the crest and culmination of a long, slow, upward sweep of recovery, the origin of which was far away at the very beginnings of that sixth century that saw the ending of one era, the opening of another. When, at the hands of the Pope, he was crowned Emperor of the West, on Christmas Day, A.D. 800 in St. Peter's, the highest point was reached in the five-century era we call roughly the Dark Ages. After his death, fourteen years later, the curve began to decline until it sunk again as low as before, in order that once more, the five-hundred-year vibration being accomplished, a new rise might be initiated that for its own period of an identical number of years, should mark the achievement, yet in the end the inevitable loss, of all Charlemagne had striven to attain.

He was the first great builder for five centuries; but of all the work in which he

was personally interested — churches, monasteries, palaces — nothing remains but the
royal chapel at Aix-la-Chapelle, and this
outwardly, and in a measure internally, has
been radically rebuilt. His secretary, Eberhard, built a small church at Steinbach
which, shorn of its aisles, still remains in a
ruinous and desecrated condition, and a few
years later St. Michael's, Fulda, was
erected. The interesting gateway and
chapel at Lorsch is fifty years later in date.
In France the baptistery of St. Jean, Poitiers, and the unique church of Germigny-
des-Prés are about all we have. How much
has been destroyed that would be illuminating on the point of architectural development, it is impossible to say, but there is
little in what remains that would indicate
irreparable loss. The chapel at Aix is
simply San Vitale at Ravenna coarsened
and largely built of old materials. It is
an octagon within an aisle of sixteen sides,
with a square presbytery, two staircase
towers, and a rectangular tribune: the vaulting of the aisles is without ribs, and the
windows are round arched and splayed.
Of course the dome, gables, towers, and
accessories are comparatively modern addi-

tions. Einhard is usually said to have been the "architect," but Rivoira questions this, making him a kind of clerk of the works, the master-builder having come from Byzantium, with, working under him, Italian craftsmen and local Frankish labourers. Steinbach is equally unimaginative and even more primitive, a T-cross plan with aisles and a semicircular apse, the simplest form of Roman basilica, translated into the rough materials of a northern and barbarous land. Germigny-des-Prés is a curious cross-shaped plan in a square enclosing nave, with a small apse terminating each of the four arms. The plan is remotely Byzantine, but the exterior composition with its central tower, its gables, and its lean-to aisles is essentially northern in expression and in a distant sort of way may be considered, if not the prototype, at least the first hesitating step in the direction of the development that three centuries later was to begin in power and end in the unexampled nobility of the Gothic church. The interesting and even original decorative scheme of inlaid stonework at Lorsch and at Poitiers with its abortive pilasters and triangular windows and steep decorative gables, is also of the north, but it never led anywhere and is no more than the sport of ambitious incompetence.

Charlemagne neither invented nor re-created a style: what he did was simply to stimulate into activity the moribund traditions of building, and as well the inheritors of these traditions. There were still in Ravenna the descendants of earlier and more competent craftsmen; the Lombards had built up a building trade of sorts and these men were undoubtedly eager for an opportunity to show what they could do. Finally, and most important of all, were the Comacini. This mysterious guild is first referred to by name in the Code of King Rotharis, the Lombard, in the year 640, but after a manner that proves a long prior existence, and a century later King Liutprand in an official memorandum, recognizes in detail the dignity and importance of its members even above all other of his Italian subjects. There is little doubt that these Comacini were the lineal successors of the old Roman building guilds, some members of which had fled to Como after the final ruin of the Empire and had preserved somewhat of their organization and of their methods and traditions, handing them down to successive generations though with constantly weakening force. It is possible that they were the progenitors of the order of Freemasons, but in any case they represent the most vigorous survival of the Roman building guilds and served to preserve some part of the old tradition while they contributed such architecture as was possible during the Dark Ages, until a new vitality in the world made inevitable a new art that was based on the very principles and methods they had saved from the general wreck.

The Comacini were a true building guild of masons, joiners, stone carvers; organized in lodges, with their apprentices, workmen, and masters. Traditionally the north Italian lakes were their habitat, but they journeyed from place to place to undertake such small work as the times might demand. For several centuries they learned nothing and forgot much. From the great days of the Baths of Diocletian — that most amazing building that contains in embryo so many of the structural elements of Mediæval architecture — to such poor little half barbarous efforts as Toscanella, is a fall indeed, but it is something that even this was possible considering that civilization itself had ceased, and Toscanella, with the similar work of the school of Ravenna, in eastern Italy and Dalmatia, was not only the last word in a long decline but the first of a still more amazing advance that rose at last to a point where even the Baths of Diocletian were immeasurably surpassed.

What these building guilds did was to standardize architecture along simple lines that fitted the time; but while it so lost all vitality it gained in two directions: first, by being held always to a standard that, while low and tending always lower, was definitely higher than the apology for civilization in which it was immersed; second, through the purging away of that artificial and illogical formalism that had been the last estate of a great art of building. What happens when a once noble art dissolves at last and no body of men remains to preserve traditions and hold to standards, we can see here in America between the years 1835 and 1885. Nothing quite so bad as this occurred in Europe during the Dark Ages, and for this we must thank the Comacini and their fellows. We can also see in the so-called "classical" architecture of the nineteenth

century in Europe as well as America, what
equally happens when life has gone out of a
style, leaving it a mass of artificial dogmas
and prejudices, and when material prosperity, instead of ruin and desolation, forms its
environment. If ease and peace and plenty
had followed the last decadence of Roman
art it is hard to see how art itself could ever
have happened again. As it was the non-
sense was completely knocked out of it by
adversity: for three centuries it was architecture reduced to its lowest terms, which
is a very good thing for this or any other
art — or society itself, for that matter —
whenever a drastic reform is imperative.

In estimating the work of this period
from the fall of Rome to the beginning of
the " Great Recovery " in the eleventh century, when nearly all the structural features
that underlie the great Gothic of the Middle
Ages were to take form and shape, it must
always be remembered that we are dealing
with only a casual few of the structures that
once existed. It is very tempting to
work assiduously backward year after year
through half forgotten fragments, finding
at last the one where first appears some
pregnant device later to achieve immortal-

[53]

ity in a Durham or a Notre Dame, and to hail this as the actual work of genius from which so much was to follow. For one such monument that remains an hundred have been destroyed to tantalize us by their bare foundations, like St. Martin of Tours, for instance, that owes its destruction to the insanity of the French Revolution. What may have been here in these ruined sanctuaries no one can say, but at least there is evidence to prove not only that Gothic did not spring full-fledged from the marvellous half century between 1150 and 1200, but that the various elements that make up its organism were either the result of a slow development extending over centuries, or of the return to far-away types suggested at least in the later architecture of Rome itself. For this reason the quarrel as to which church possesses the earliest ribbed vault is little to the point. It may be Montefiascone, or Sant' Ambrogio, or Durham, but may perfectly well have been any one of another score of French or Lombard churches, no vestige of which now remains; moreover the fact still confronts us that in Syria, and even in the later buildings of the Roman Empire, ribbed vaults were used, and their reappearance in the eleventh century may be the result either of reinvention or of rediscovery of precedents long forgotten.

The question therefore suggests itself: May we not, in pronouncing the work of the Dark Ages generally barren and retrogressive, be doing it injustice, just because the great mass of building has been utterly destroyed? The chance is negligible, for the chapel at Aix remains and San Lorenzo Maggiore, Milan, in its plan and general structure, and we know that both were lauded by contemporary chroniclers as crowning and incredible triumphs of art. Undoubtedly they represent the best work possible to the Comacine guilds of the north, as Sant' Apollinare in Classe, Parenzo, and Pomposa were the best the successors of the guilds of Ravenna could produce in their own territory, and on this basis we can only estimate the architecture of the sixth and seventh centuries as dry, lifeless, and without invention, yet possessed of a certain naïve seriousness and self-respect that enlist our sympathy if they cannot win our admiration.

Two general plans were in vogue and

employed indifferently as between the region architecturally subject to Ravenna and that which fell to the lot of the Comacine masters: the basilica and the aisled and domed polygon. The basilica was the original Roman hall, with its two rows of columns supporting arches that bore the small-windowed clerestory, and divided the area into three sections, the central one being about double the width of the side aisles. In the simplest form the nave proper ends in a semicircular apse surmounted by a half dome, smaller apses for side altars being added later as terminations of the aisles. The central area was covered by a trussed roof of timber, the side aisles by lean-to roofs, and there were neither towers, domes, nor masonry vaults. As the churches grew in size an aisleless transept was added between nave and apse to give space for richer ceremonial, greater numbers of clergy or monks, and for additional altars. So came the T-cross plan which is the basis of all Mediæval church plans. This basilican type was practically universal under Constantine, and in the end it won, during the Dark Ages, supremacy in the west, quite displacing the circular or polygonal type.

This latter had an eventful career. Its prototype may be found in certain Roman tombs and great apartments in the Imperial baths, though the analogy is somewhat strained, and the relation between the calidarium of the Baths of Caracalla and San Vitale is far to seek. The first is simply a circular hall enclosed by enormously thick walls in which square and semicircular niches are cut, and surmounted by a low, ponderous dome: it is without any particular articulation and is quite static in quality. The second is highly organized, with the load concentrated on massive piers, between which little arcaded apses project into an intricately vaulted, surrounding aisle of two superimposed stories. One of these apses is thrust through the aisle until it projects beyond the perimeter of the aisle wall. The central polygon rises well above the aisles and is covered by a hemispherical dome which is supported by large arches subdivided by columns into three spaces also covered by arches: altogether a very rich and highly articulated scheme unlike anything Rome can offer in comparison. It seems to me an undoubted fact that the polygonal and domical church is a development of the East, probably in the dioceses of Damascus and Antioch, and brought thence to Constantinople and Ravenna by master builders who we know were continually drawn from this section by the Emperors of the East.

Whatever its source it was the chief factor in the development of the supreme architecture of the reign of Justinian, and through San Vitale, Aix-la-Chapelle and Sta. Maria Maggiore, Milan, had everything to do with the evolution of the Gothic chevet, as I shall try to show later. In itself, as the general scheme for a church, it found scant favour in the West, yielding place to the basilican form, which had established itself in Rome, had already gone thence with the spreading of Christianity, and was by nature capable of almost indefinite expansion in all directions.

Throughout the Dark Ages, then, this basilican form, reduced to its lowest terms, was the standard of building. The vast majesty of the Constantinian churches in Rome, the marble and mosaic splendours of the Constantinople of Justinian, the more sober richness of the Ravenna of the exarchs were very far away, and in their place we have rough masonry of brick and stone, small round-arched windows with splayed reveals, misfit marble columns, with odds and ends of capitals left from ruined buildings, and exteriors unornamented except for narrow pilaster strips, arched corbel courses, and sometimes, as at Agliate and San Vincenzo in Prato, rude arcades built up on the haunches of semi-domes to support the protecting roofs.

Of ornamental carving there is more than one might expect, but it usually appears in altar fronts and canopies, and in tombs. It is very flat, very conventionalized, yet decorative and with a curiously delicate feeling for space composition. The symbolism is conservatively Early Christian, the motives decadent Byzantine with curious Syrian admixtures, and here and there, as in the increasing frequency of dragons and wild beasts and birds, something that is essentially of the north. It is only here, however, that the new barbarian blood begins to show itself; structurally and in point of architectural design the northern races, in spite of their universal dominion, exert no influence whatever. The slowly expiring tradition of Rome, Ravenna, and Byzan-

tium is still in full control, and it is not until
the beginning of the eleventh century (that
mystical year 1000, when the world awakes
to new possibilities and begins the development of the greatest era in history) that the
tribes of the north, Christianized, brought
into orderly association, and subjected to
the vital stimulus of a regenerated monasticism, begin to raise the fabric of their
own self-expression on the foundations furnished for them by the humble builders of
the Dark Ages. It has been a long period
of five centuries of arduous growth, not
into civilization but toward it. They had
destroyed the classical culture of Rome as
they had devastated her cities, but instead
of inheriting her wealth and acquiring ease
and plenty they had found themselves heirs
to poverty, anarchy, and desolation. One
thing they had gained which had been no
part of their plan, and that was Christianity; and the Church, standing for five hundred years before their eyes as the one
centre of certainty in a wilderness of change
and hopeless disorder, had, through her
monks and missionaries, subjected them to
new influences that in the end must bear
fruit in a new culture, a new civilization,

a new righteousness, and therefore a new art. What the results were we shall try to see when we take up in our next lecture the story of amazing advance from the millennial year that saw the Dark Ages end and the great Catholic Middle Ages begin their triumphant career.

LECTURE III

THE GREAT AWAKENING

THE Carolingian renaissance was short-lived: there was always something artificial and predetermined about it, and it outlived the great Emperor scarcely a generation. Fourteen years after the crowning in St. Peter's, he was dead and succeeded by his son, Louis the Pious, who was ill-fitted for those strenuous times. Royal quarrels wrecked the unstable Empire, and at the Treaty of Verdun it fell apart, rent vertically between France, Lorraine and Italy, and Germany, the second division then including all of what is now France east of the Rhone and Germany west of the Rhine, while Germany itself extended only as far as the Elbe in the north, the Danube and Save in the south. Brandenburg, Pomerania, and Prussia were still entirely barbarian, and destined to remain so for four centuries.

The decline in culture and civilization was instant and headlong: war and anarchy took the place of order, morals degenerated, and once more savage invaders — Northmen in France, Huns in Germany — pushed on across the dissolving frontiers carrying fire and death and leaving wide ruin behind them. It was bad enough in France where the Vikings from their long ships were sweeping all the north and sailing up the Seine to sack and burn Rouen and Paris, and in Germany where the Huns were following suit, but it was worst of all in Italy, for there the collapse of society was most complete. The degradation of morals was so flagrant that at last the general corruption infected even the Church, which, already rent by the Eastern schism in 866, sank to the lowest point in its history. There were of course good bishops, priests, and especially monks, who had not abandoned themselves to simony, pluralism, and debauchery, but the rule was otherwise, and for years even the chair of Peter was filled by laymen and simoniacal priests who had won their places through bribery, corruption, and murder, and even, for one incredible period, by the bastards and favourites of the unspeakable Marozia and her Roman clan.

If the Carolingian epoch was the "false dawn" of Christian civilization, the last half of the ninth century and the first quarter of the tenth formed that darkest period of night that comes just before the real dawn. For the dawn came, in the midst of a tempest of destruction, horror, and humiliation; came as irresistibly as the rising of the sun, and, it would seem, as independently of human control. Just why this sudden and unpredicted regeneration should then have shown itself with power is hard to say. It is sufficiently easy to understand why the eleventh century should have begun in vigour to close in glory, for by that time all things had been prepared, but why out of the horror of the ninth century should suddenly arise the first beginnings in the tenth is one of those phenomena that baffle the understanding of evolutionists and are comprehensible only to those who believe that the destinies of the world are under the guidance and control of a Supreme Omniscience Who walks not by the ways of man but otherwise.

In any case the change occurred and with startling suddenness and energy. The first significant event, marking the sharp transi-

[64]

tion from one century to another, is the founding of the monastery of Cluny in 909. Since the establishing of the Order of St. Benedict nothing so pregnant of possibilities for the future had taken place. Cluny was Benedictinism, reformed, regenerated, and showing itself in different guise, but the legitimate successor of the earlier monasticism, and in itself, and through its offshoot, the Cistercian Order, was to act as the spiritual stimulus of Europe for two centuries and make possible the great epoch of Mediævalism.

The Cluniac Rule was promulgated in 927, by Abbot Odo, and from that date Cluny became an operative and dominant force. In the meantime secular events of equal importance had taken place, for in 919 Henry the Fowler began the Saxon line that was to lead to Otto the Great, and the resurrected Holy Roman Empire. In England the work and character of Alfred the Great were bearing fruit in a rapid increase in culture, craftsmanship, learning, and international influence, with St. Dunstan as a type of the time and a kind of patron saint of all the arts from architecture to embroidery. In a way, however,

Alfred must be looked on as a later counterpart of Charlemagne, embodying as he did the low cresting of the wave of the Dark Ages, from 500 to 1000, rather than the first evidences of the new life that was to mark the succeeding epoch. His own era of advancement was short-lived; the Danish invasions followed, with a consequent period of retrogression, and the real era of Mediævalism was not to begin until the Norman Conquest of 1066, a full century later than the beginnings on the Continent.

In 936 Otto the Great became Emperor and under his firm hand the Hungarians and Slavs were beaten back, new regions were brought under western influence, Christianity crossed over the borders of heathen neighbours, and the new power, order, and dignity of the Teutonic empire led inevitably to the union of Germany and Italy and the founding of the Holy Roman Empire of the Germanic peoples. Hugh Capet in 987 wrote " finis " at the end of the line of degenerate Carolingians and established the Capetian dynasty, while Denmark in 935 and Poland in 966 had accepted Christianity and marked their submission by enthroning Christian kings.

Nor must the influence of the Arabs be disregarded. From their capitol at Cordova, a centre of education, learning, science, and culture, a vital and stimulating force had extended itself over all western Europe, curiously combining with the new Catholic and monastic spirit, to give a fresh impetus to renascent civilization. Finally, in the very last year of the tenth century, the degradation of the Papacy received its first check through Pope Sylvester II, who was followed by Benedict VIII, and, after the scandalous relapse of John XIX and Benedict IX, by such great leaders and true shepherds as Clement II, Leo IX, and Hildebrand Pope Gregory VII, the last one of the very great figures in history and the corner-stone of the Mediæval Church.

From the beginning the monks of Cluny had been the chief influence toward righteousness, steadfast even when the Papacy itself was renegade and rotten, and in the end lifting it to their own lofty plane of thought, conduct, and action. Partly because of this faithfulness (which was preserved and even intensified by the succeeding Cistercians, Carthusians, and Augustinians, and even later by the Dominicans and Franciscans), the " regulars " or monastic clergy not only acquired power and influence, together with the confidence and affection of the people, far above that of the secular or parochial clergy, but they dominated and controlled the episcopate and even the Papacy itself. For a time Cluny was more powerful than the Pope, and so was Clairvaux in its turn, and as the first took charge of the Normans, Christianizing them and making Normandy the greatest centre of energy in Europe, so the second seized upon the Franks and gave to them the task, and the ability to accomplish it, of perfecting what Normandy had initiated.

Between them they created the Christian civilization of the Middle Ages, monasticism in two diverse forms working through two races of diverse blood, but both essentially of the north; Norman on the one hand, French and Burgundian on the other. The expression of this civilization in artistic form was, first, Norman architecture, second, the Gothic architecture of the Île de France.

The experience of every student of Mediævalism is, I think, a first return to

the thirteenth century as the centre of interest and enthusiasm, then an immediate
working back to the twelfth century as
representing something far more massive,
vigorous, and significant, and finally an
almost enforced return to the eleventh century. The thirteenth, well called by Dr.
Walsh " the greatest of centuries," was an
era of glorious accomplishment, but in it
were already showing the first evidences of
dissolution. The twelfth was the century
of magnificent endeavour, and all that was
great in its successor is here in embryo, not
alone in art but in philosophy, religion, and
the conduct of life. The eleventh century
is a time of aspiration and of vision, of the
enunciation of new principles and of the
first shock of contest between the old that
was doomed, the new that was destined to
unprecedented victories. Great leaders
suddenly arise out of an age without leaders: Henry II, Henry IV, Edmund Iron-
sides, Edward the Confessor, William the
Conqueror, Boleslav of Poland, Olaf of
Sweden, Sancho the Great of Navarre,
Pope Sylvester II, Leo IX, Gregory VII,
St. Anselm, Lanfranc, St. Peter Damian,
Fulbert of Chartres, Bernward of Hildes-

heim, Guido Arretino, Avicenna; monasteries and convents on the reformed lines of Cluny were springing up on every hand, redeeming the wilderness, spreading education, establishing works of mercy and charity.

The civilization of the eleventh century was monastic, feudal, and predominantly Norman. Its vitality was prodigious. At every point the heathen assaults had been beaten back, the peril of the false prophet was apparently at an end, and the northern tribes, whether Teutonic, Norse, Saxon, or Frank, had been Christianized and partly assimilated, excepting always the still heathen tribes of Prussia and Brandenburg. Feudalism had saved Europe with the aid of St. Benedict and his monks: now the reformed Benedictines of Cluny were to redeem it, with the Christianized Vikings of Normandy as their efficient arm. Originally the most savage of peoples they had perforce followed their Duke Richard when he accepted Christianity in 961, and in two generations had become the most zealous and active adherents of the Church. In the first half of the eleventh century, twenty great monasteries, including three of world-

wide influence (Bec, Fécamp, and Jumièges), were founded in Normandy alone,
and into Britain, Italy, Sicily, the Levant,
streamed the Norman adventurers, light-
heartedly, high-handedly, seizing on degenerate counties and dukedoms, cutting out
new kingdoms for themselves and generally
becoming both a public nuisance and an
agency of regeneration.

It must all have been very unpleasant for
the upholders of the *ancien régime,* the
simoniacal Popes, absentee bishops, and
married or profligate clergy; for the degenerate feudal lords, the *fainéant* kings, and
the Emperors both of the West and the East
who had, as they thought, safely brought
the great engine of the Church under their
direct and personal control. Never was
such an upheaval, such a rattling of the dry
bones of wide decrepitude by militant
monks hot with the zeal of reform, and
Norman, Frankish, and Flemish adventurers whose headstrong careers were em-
bellished by an equally headstrong religious
ardour. In the end Europe proved too
small for the exuberant vitality of a north
that suddenly had found itself, and the riot
of action culminated, just as the century

closed, in the astonishing spectacle of the First Crusade.

Of course art answered to the exciting stimulus, as it always does when the driving impulse is based on fundamental things. Music, from about 1030, developed on new and brilliant lines; at the very beginning of the century nuns in their Rhenish cloisters were writing Latin comedies; in Hildesheim and Liége the arts of metal achieved a sudden and amazing splendour, sculpture began its recovery in the south of France, while architecture opened like an expanding flower, not only in Normandy, but in France, Burgundy, the Rhineland, and every quarter of Italy from Lombardy to Calabria and Sicily.

Three tendencies show themselves, or rather we should say, three schools develop, for the tendency of all was at first the same, though one of the schools was short-lived and played little part in the later developments of the other two which, merged at last, furnished all of Gothic except the vitalizing spirit. These three schools were those of Tuscany, Lombardy, and Normandy. The first, which was sporadic and of very brief duration, is mysterious and almost inexplicable, and is represented, amongst existing buildings, by San Miniato and the Baptistery in Florence, and, in a measure, by Pisa Cathedral. This work is generally included under the generic title " Lombard," but this seems to me a mistake, for it is structurally and æsthetically different from the true Lombard work of the same period. Certain common elements are visible, for example, qualities that are conspicuously Syrian, but the things that, in Lombard architecture, are traceable to Ravenna, or to the Comacine guilds, do not appear at all. Structurally this Tuscan work is static, while its rival is constantly progressing through one experiment after another until it arrives at a point where its new and pregnant devices are taken over by the Franks and made into Gothic. In craftsmanship it is vastly superior to the nascent art of the Lombards, clean-cut, delicate, classical, while its inlaid, polychromatic ornament is in a class by itself. You cannot call it Ravennesque, still less can you call it Byzantine; in a sense it is classical Greek, though strongly modified by an Eastern influence and adapted to the new environment of a Christian society. Bishop

Hildebrand began San Miniato in 1013, but there is no record of the name of the master builder. He could have been no local genius, for no building exists in Tuscany, or has been recorded, that resembles it in the least. It is not a direct successor of the Roman basilica, for it shows an articulation of a high order and is manifestly the result of many generations of development. It bears not the slightest relation to Toscanella, and as for the Comacini, a glance at Sant' Abondio, Como, exactly contemporary in date, dispels all thought of authorship on their part. It seems to be the work of some Greek artist from Syria, for with its division into three square bays of three arched openings each, separated by piers carrying transverse arches across nave and aisles alike, it has a close resemblance to certain ruined churches of the diocese of Antioch of a period antedating the work of Justinian at Constantinople. The Florentine Baptistery is of the same temper, Syrian Greek as opposed both to Byzantium and Ravenna; but the Duomo of Pisa, while Syrian in plan and containing many Hellenic qualities, is also touched by Lombard influences. Pisa is the direct prototype of that very beau-

tiful round-arched style of the Italian thirteenth century which is the true " Gothic "
or Mediæval expression of Italy, rather
than the superficially Gothic incidents that
are so generally unsuccessful and are usually taken to express this particular period.

This combination of Greek and Syrian
influences is what one would have expected,
for Constantinople and Syria were still the
leading centres of culture in the world,
apart from the Arabs, who, as infidels, were
formal enemies. During the era of the
Ottos the connection between the Empire
and the East was very close, while southern
Italy was still an appanage of Constantinople. The Empress Theophano was a
daughter of the Eastern Emperor, wife of
Otto II and mother of Otto III. In her
train came artisans and artists of all kinds
from Constantinople, and great stores of
woven and embroidered stuffs, metal work,
and carved ivories. Great as was this influence from the Bosporus, that which fil-
tered in from Syria was of equal magnitude,
and, at least so far as southern France was
concerned, even more penetrating and permanent in its effects.

All through the Dark Ages Syria was the

most fertile and wealthy province of the
Eastern Empire and the Syrian merchants
were the chief Mediterranean navigators.
Through Marseilles and Arles these merchants with their ivories, stuffs, jewels, and
wines, worked their way into all parts of
Gaul and even into the valley of the Rhine,
making permanent settlements not only in
the towns of Provence but in Worms, Metz,
Cologne. One rather gathers from St.
Jerome and Salvianno and Gregory of
Tours that they were somewhat of a nuisance, as they were clannish, industrious,
and inordinately avaricious. Whatever
wealth there was seems to have been largely
concentrated in their hands, but at least
they played a powerful part in the development of art when it began to recover itself
in the eleventh century, though their contributions were purely decorative, and had
little to do with the great structural revolution that was begun by the Lombards,
continued by the Normans and completed
by the French.

Certain of these decorative importations
may well be the norm of definite Gothic
devices, as, for example, crockets, which
were long supposed to be Teutonic in their

origin, but which are to be found in Carolingian illuminations almost copied from
such Syrian manuscripts as the Rabula
Gospels. The twin flanking towers of the
west front of churches may be traced directly back from Coutances and York
through the Norman abbeys, to Como and
Sant' Ambrogio, and through ivories, gems,
and miniatures of the fifth century and of
Syrian workmanship, to Syria itself, where
they form the established type.

The second school is that of Lombardy,
interesting, vital, and significant. If San
Pietro, Toscanella, is really eighth century
even in part, it is one of the earliest buildings of this style, though its strikingly
beautiful façade must be credited to a
period nearly five centuries later when it
attained its highest point. The church at
Agliate is a century later and San Vincenzo in Prato, Milan, of the same date,
i.e. the first half of the ninth century. Then
in steady progression come such architecturally and archæologically important monuments as Sant' Eustorgio, Milan; Santo Ste-
fano, Verona; Sant' Abondio, Como; San
Flaviano, Montefiascone; and Sant' Ambrogio, Milan. Now, the earliest of these are

[77]

of the Dark Ages, and in them is no sign of life or invention, but from Sant' Eustorgio onward the churches I have named are all of the eleventh century and in one or the other may be found the earliest stages in the working out of many of the structural features that conditioned the Gothic style of architecture. Here, in this brief space of time, we may find the full development of the compound pier from the cylindrical column, the alternating system, the concentration of loads and thrusts with their necessary buttresses, the pointed, ribbed, and domical vault, and even the beginnings of the chevet itself.

This development of the original basilican plan and organism until it finally culminated at the hands of other races and far in the north, was somewhat as follows:

The supply of ancient marble columns being exhausted, circular or square piers built up of small stones were substituted. At about the same time arches were thrown across the aisles from each pier to the outer wall, possibly for æsthetic reasons, more probably for purposes of stability. In any case they involved the addition of a pilaster to the pier to take the arch on its inner side, and so the first step toward the compound pier was accomplished. Next, great and high arches were flung across the nave, partly for stability, partly because of their beauty. These arches were either on every third pier, as at San Miniato, or on every alternate pier. In either case an additional pilaster was built on the pier that bore the nave arch, so making it cruciform, while the intermediate support, having less work to do, was made smaller. Thus the alternating system of the late Norman and early Gothic was begun, while the scaffolding had been prepared for the next innovation, which was masonry vaulting. This began first in the small areas of the side aisles, and was plainly groined, without ribs. Almost immediately the structural convenience of ribs was either rediscovered or remembered from the Baths of Diocletian, or copied from Syria, and after this the whole scheme of Gothic construction was inevitable. The ribs made elaborate centring no longer necessary, since they were built first and then the spaces simply filled with thin stones from the haunch upward. This simplification made the high vault possible, and this at first was quadripartite, or just the space of two of the aisle arches. Which was the first ribbed and pointed nave vault is a question that is archæological rather than architectural. That it was not earlier than 1025 or later than 1075 we are reasonably sure. The vault of Sant' Ambrogio is of the year 1060 and so perfect it is surely not the first. Venturi, Stiehl, Lethaby believe this ribbed, pointed, and domed vault to be a Norman invention, and others claim that Durham in England is the first. It does not really matter, the feat had been accomplished, and that is really all we need to know.

Already we have a definite concentration of loads on certain points, and æsthetic recognition of this new principle. This involved a new scheme of buttressing, for while the thick Roman walls of the aisles had served to take the thrust of the transverse aisle arches, the nave arches, particularly when stone vaults were added, were a different matter. Naturally the first step was to build transverse walls across the aisles, piercing these with arched openings, as at Sant' Ambrogio. This is as far as the Lombards went; the flying buttress was the final structural refinement of the Normans and the Franks.

The chevet, the development of which is an interesting and rather special story, I shall take up later. The Lombards ventured a few tentative steps in this direction, but the real work was apparently done farther north, and is twelfth century rather than eleventh.

Æsthetically the Lombards were as successful as they were structurally. The great glory of the style they had initiated was to come in the twelfth century in the churches of Modena, Pavia, Parma, Murano, and in the thirteenth century in Pisa, Lucca, Pistoja, but even in the eleventh century the self-restrained simplicity of the ordinary exteriors, with their narrow pilaster strips, corbelled cornices, simple round-arched windows, and primitive apse arcades, is very notable.

It is an interesting and a significant fact that as in the north the rebirth of culture and civilization is directly traceable to the great spiritual awakening that took form and shape in Cluny, so here in Italy the growth of a new art is consonant with a similar religious revival, stimulated by

Cluny itself, though following a somewhat different and less permanent form of development. Cluny was based on the " community spirit" and was made up of self-contained groups of men united under one rule. In Italy the horrors of the tenth century drove thinking and righteous men out of the world and into the wilderness as hermits, and though the influence of these pious anchorites was enormous it was personal only and could not outlast their lives. St. Nilus of Calabria and St. Romuald of Ravenna are types of the holy men of the time, and the latter, says Villari, made Ravenna for a time almost a rival in sanctity of Cluny itself. Princes, patricians, a Doge of Venice, St. Adalbert of Bohemia (who was martyred by the heathen Prussians he had laboured to convert) sought in the far solitudes release from the intolerable oppression of social degeneration; and they, with Gerbert, Bishop of Ravenna after 998, exerted a vast influence for good on the second and third Ottos as Holy Roman Emperors. St. Romuald, in fact, had hopes of inducing Otto III to renounce the crown of empire and become a hermit, but for once he failed, and this prince, who through his enlightenment and spiritual fervour might have been the regenerator of Europe in its civil aspect, died at the age of twenty-two, followed two months later by Pope Sylvester, Otto's counterpart in the Church, and disorder reigned again. The impulse had been sufficient however, and now in Italy, as in Normandy, to quote the contemporary monk, Rudolf of Cluny, " It was as though the earth, rousing itself and casting away its ancient vesture, clothed itself with the white robe of churches."

The third school is that of Normandy. It owes nothing to the *neo-Grec* episode of Tuscany, but it took over all the Lombard school and, striking out for itself, by the vigour of the new northern blood and the impulse and insistence of Cluny, assembled it all, organized it in a splendid coherency, carried each new thing to a logical conclusion, supplemented these by additional devices of the highest genius, and finally handed the whole noble work to the Franks and their Cistercian guides to be raised to the highest point of logical articulation and given that distinct and unique æsthetic quality that fixed in everlasting form the Gothic style.

In searching for the earliest beginnings of this era-making work we are grievously handicapped by the gross and wanton sacrilege of the French Revolution. Innumerable great works of the noblest art suffered total destruction during the eighteenth century anarchy; amongst them three of unique value both artistically and archæologically: Cluny, Saint-Benigne of Dijon; and Saint-Martin of Tours. A fourth in the sequence, Jumièges, was also shattered and laid desolate by the same *sans-culottes,* but fortunately still remains as a majestical ruin, while Cérisy-la-Forêt was by some miracle overlooked.

The name and personality of the first of the great line of builders, and himself the greatest of all, are known and should be honoured by all architects. William of Volpiano was born in 961 on a little island of Lake Orta in Italy. When very young he became a monk of Cluny, then at the age of twenty-nine Abbot of Saint-Benigne, Dijon, and a few years later, at the personal solicitation of Richard II of Normandy, Abbot of Fécamp. Filled with the most ardent zeal for the reformation of morals, both secular and religious, he was apparently a master builder — or, as we should say, architect — of amazing ability. The lost abbey of Dijon was his work, also the abbey church of Bernay (now desecrated, partially razed, and used for all manner of base purposes), Frutuaria in Italy, and a number of destroyed and less important monuments. The original abbey church at Mont-Saint-Michel was constructed during his lifetime and under the direction of his disciple, Abbot Hildebert II; Cérisy-la-Forêt by the famous monk Durandus, also a disciple, and by Almodus, who had been clerk of the works at Mont-Saint-Michel. Jumièges, if not his actual creation, was built under his influence by yet another apt pupil, Robert II, then abbot, and afterward both Bishop of London and Archbishop of Canterbury. Finally the pregnant transitional work of the early twelfth century was under the inspiration of Lanfranc, who, born at Pavia in 1005, became a monk of Bec in 1042, only nine years after the death of William of Volpiano.

The loss of Saint-Benigne is irreparable: it marked the first advent in the north of the Lombard principles; it formed the point of contact between Italy and France, and, judging from its foundations, which are all the revolutionists have left us, and from most defective drawings, it was an unique stage in the development of the Gothic chevet. It was a T-cross basilica, with apse and flanking absidioles; a great circular church or rotunda adjoined it to the east, and by two rings of columns was divided into a central well with two vaulted galleries, while again to the east was a quadrangular chapel forming the tomb of the saint. The importance of this building cannot be overestimated, and a glance at the conjectural plan will show how, in the year 1002, it amazingly foreshadows the fully developed cathedral of the thirteenth century. Undoubtedly its resemblance to the Church of the Holy Sepulchre in Jerusalem links it also with the school of Syria.

Bernay, constructed in 1013, is the true beginning of the Norman style, lofty, massive, masculine: a Latin cross with deep chancel (instead of the Italian T-cross), with compound piers and archivolts, ambulatories in the thickness of the walls, and the full order of arcade, triforium, and clerestory, though the triforium arches were later blocked up. Mont-Saint-Michel is next in order, and proceeds in richness and articulation beyond Bernay, from which it was copied, while here for the first time the walls are reduced in thickness and buttresses are substituted — a vital change, the significance of which is inestimable.

Cérisy-la-Forêt and Jumièges supplement each other, for in the former the west front and towers, with five bays of the nave, have been destroyed, while in the latter the original apse was supplanted by an elaborate chevet in the fourteenth century, and this wholly disappeared at the Revolution, leaving hardly more than the nave and west front structurally intact. These two churches are momentous in the history of architectural development. Cérisy is articulated beyond everything achieved before; it is a Latin cross with a polygonal apse, wide transepts, and aisled nave and choir. It looks to be of the same date as Saint Georges de Boscherville, and therefore later than Jumièges, but this does not help us much, since it is not sure whether the former church is of 1050 or 1110. It certainly is more delicate in design than Jumièges, but on the other hand the aisles and triforia of Jumièges are vaulted, which is a sign of increasing confidence and ability on the part of its creators. Rivoira is explicit in his statement that it was consecrated in 1032 and that Durandus was the architect: on the other hand Rupricht Robert dates it 1150, and Porter comes between with a guess at 1130. From the evidence of the building itself I should incline to the very end of the eleventh century. In any case it is a very noble work of art with many elements of transcending importance, e.g. the alternating system with transverse nave arches at every other pier, the apse with three stories of windows and wall passages at the two upper levels, and the finely developed square central tower. If it is earlier than Jumièges, it is the first church in the north to adopt the Lombard transverse arches across the nave, — the first step toward the Gothic high vault and the sexpartite form; if later, then the same is true of Jumièges, which was certainly built in 1040. In both cases all the previous steps toward the development of the Gothic system have been brought together, while the proportions have become lofty and noble, the parts admirably related, and the whole infused with a certain poetical quality

hitherto unknown. I am persuaded that
Jumièges originally had alternating transverse nave arches, like Cérisy, though I believe no one has suggested this before. Its
western towers are of extraordinary beauty
of composition and outline, but the end of
the nave between is crude and undeveloped
and is, I imagine, something left over from
a much earlier church.

We are now ready to go on to the development of the true Gothic style, and in
doing so I shall deliberately transfer to the
next lecture consideration of the Norman
churches of Lanfranc and after, for even
if they fall within the eleventh century and
are in themselves the crowning of the Norman style, they are also precisely those
structures in which the principle of dead
loads is being transformed into that of concentrated weights and living thrusts, therefore an essential part of the development
of the earliest Gothic.

First, however, a word should be given to
two other local types of architecture in this
very wonderful eleventh century, though
neither ever had any distinctive influence
in the later and perfected art of Europe.
These are the Venetian school and that of

the Rhine. In Venice the weaving of the "white robe of churches" gave us that immortal concentration of beauty, San Marco, through an apparently deliberate rejection of both the Ravenna and the Lombard schools and a return to Byzantium, for the church itself was a fairly close copy of the Church of the Holy Apostles of Justinian. This strong Eastern influence persisted in Venice quite through the Middle Ages, resulting in a local architecture of exquisite beauty, secular as well as religious. By some sport of fancy the same model was followed at Saint-Front, Périgueux, while the Venetian influence extended to Padua on the mainland, and across the Adriatic to the Dalmatian colonies. Beautiful as it all was it was outside the line of European development, and whenever, as at Padua, it tried to adapt itself to other conditions it lost all vitality and rapidly died in a condition of dull inertia. Later, in Sicily, under the stimulating influence of the Norman conquerors, similar Byzantine motives were adopted with brilliant results, but here also the effect was confined within the island walls and did not extend itself either geographically or in point of time.

In the Rhineland the year 1000 brought
the same revival that it miraculously seemed
to confer on the rest of Europe.. Otto III
was emperor, the Italian influence increasingly powerful, while Cluny was as operative as elsewhere. As we have seen, the
Syrian element was strong all through the
Rhineland, the Empress-Mother, Theophano, had all the love for beauty of her
native East, while much of the Comacine
work of Charlemagne was still standing as
a series of models. In general the eleventh
century building was not notably differentiated from that in Lombardy, Burgundy,
and Normandy, and such a church as St.
Michael's, Hildesheim, is quite capable of
holding its own with the best these countries
could show during the first quarter of the
eleventh century. The same is true of
St. Maria im Capitol, the plan of which is
quite unique, with apsidal terminations for
the choir and both transepts and aisles entirely encircling all three, this being the
first record of aisles carried along both sides
of the chancel and around the apse as well.
The apsidal transepts were copied once or
twice later, but they never became popular.
This is true of all the Teutonic contribu-

tions to contemporary church building. From the time of the Abbey of St. Gall it had been a German fashion to duplicate the eastern apse at the west end of the church, and sometimes the transept also: the result was a composition without unity or focus, and the miscellaneous collection of towers that inevitably followed produced a chaotic and unimpressive effect. Nothing of this extended itself either to France or England, and after its first efflorescence the Rhenish style froze into the dull severity of Speyer, Worms, Mainz, and Coblenz, a severity that broke up outside into an unintelligent chaos of towers, spires, and domes encrusted with mechanical and uninspired detail.

In itself the church building of the eleventh and twelfth centuries in the Rhineland lacked all spontaneity of structural development: ingenious in devising new combinations of apses, towers, and arcades, it contented itself with this, and with the construction of cathedrals impressive because of their colossal dimensions. The universal problem was, however, the perfecting of a scheme of construction that should be logical, organic, highly articulated, and, a little later, economical. All the materials were at hand, gathered from Syria, Ravenna, Constantinople, Rome; they had been analyzed, assorted, developed into new significance and assembled into units already showing a life and movement unknown for five centuries. The next step after development of detail and co-ordination of effort was creation, and high-heartedly the men of Normandy and Burgundy and France and England set themselves to their task.

LECTURE IV

THE EPOCH OF TRANSITION

In my last lecture I considered the brilliant achievements of the first great builder of the eleventh century in the north, William of Volpiano, and of those who immediately carried on his principles. We now must turn to a second figure of equal architectural significance, Lanfranc of Bec, who carried still further the ideas of the great master and was his immediate and most able successor. Like William he was an Italian, born in Pavia in 1005. At the age of thirty-four he went to Avranches, where he established one of the many schools of this fertile time, but almost immediately abandoned his educational work for the cloister, and became a monk of Bec in 1042. The result was momentous, for at once this minor monastery became the intellectual centre of Europe, drawing professors from every part of the west, and students in such numbers that the old buildings proved inadequate, and were at once replaced by magnificent new structures designed by Lanfranc himself — so far as we know his first essay in architecture.

It may seem to you that I disprove my own contention when I admit that the two great architectural masters in northern Europe in the eleventh century, the very men who took over the Lombard innovations and not only co-ordinated them but gave them a new and transcendent character as the logical steps toward an inevitable Gothic, were not men of the north at all but Italians, and you may say therefore that it is to Italy and the classical south, not to Normandy and the Catholic north, that credit should be given for this era-making work. It should be remembered, however, that the real creative ability in Italy was Lombard, i.e. of that region where the old Latin race had been almost wholly superseded by northern, and semi-Norse, semi-Teutonic tribes, and that William of Volpiano and Lanfranc were both undeniably of this alien blood. On the other hand it is sure that this northern force, so vast in its vigour and potentiality, would never have become operative but for the fertiliz-

ing power of the indestructible classical
tradition which had lain fallow through the
centuries of devastation, only to assert itself
with something of its old vigour when conditions had become favourable.

It is impossible too strongly to emphasize
the persistence and the beneficence of this
classical heritage, which from time to time
asserts itself through alien races and in alien
times. It came with power in the tenth
and eleventh centuries, again in the fourteenth and fifteenth, and it is no hard task
for us, today, to see its recrudescence again
after the powerfully Teutonic epoch of the
eighteenth and nineteenth centuries. Ever
since the Latin tradition was apparently
stamped out forever under the trampling
of Teutonic conquest, it has been those
peoples who were earlier under its civiliz-
ing influence that have come forward as
centres of culture and of creative force, and
of social dynamics. Italy, Spain, France,
Britain, the Rhineland, all are coheritors of
the classical tradition, and Russia herself
owes her religion, her philosophy, and her
art to that eastern Rome on the shores of
the Bosporus that, before many days, may
become the capital of a restored and even

more glorious Byzantine Empire. The eastern half of Germany, Hungary, and Scandinavia are the only countries of Europe that never knew in any degree the influence of Latin culture and civilization, and the lack can never be supplied from any human source whatever.

Again, we may admit that the blood of the Mediterranean races had exhausted itself and was no longer able to utilize its own tradition. Of its own motion the clean blood of the northern tribes could probably have done little, but the combining of the two forces, raised to creative activity by the inspiration of a vital, personal, and beautiful religion, resulted in a living force of unexampled potentiality, and the result was the culture and the philosophy and the art of Mediævalism.

William and Lanfranc, then, were the bearers of a great wonder out of Italy, but it was the lusty Normans and the ardent Franks who gave it form and life.

Not one stone remains on another of Lanfranc's new buildings at Bec, and of his abbey of the Trinité at Caen only the crypt exists, as the present church is the result of a rebuilding half a century later. The

Abbaye aux Hommes, or St. Étienne, at Caen, therefore stands as Lanfranc's first undoubted work. The easterly portion was consecrated in 1077, the western in 1081, and it was built (together with the original Trinité) by Duke William of Normandy, the " Conqueror," in expiation of some of his rebellions against ecclesiastical inhibitions. There is a tradition that the second of these churches records the remorse of the impulsive duke for his harshness to his Duchess Matilda in parading through the streets of Caen with the lady tied by the hair to the tail of his horse, as an evidence of his annoyance at her domestic conduct. This story probably does grave injustice to William as well as to the manners of the time, even though these were more forcible, direct, and unconventional than happened at a later date.

This church, while following generally the type of Jumièges, is a long step in advance, both structurally and artistically. It is a vast Latin cross, with a high and fully developed triforium gallery roofed by an half barrel vault, compound piers of richly multiplied section and on the alternating system, central and western towers, and, for the first time (if we assign to Cérisy-la-Forêt its probable later date) a conscious effort at giving to the exterior decorative architectural quality and some expression of inner organism. For the first time also we find the three west doors given an architectural character, and forming the first step toward the ultimate glory of the typical French west portals. The crude sexpartite vaulting of the nave is of the twelfth century, for while Lanfranc evidently intended to vault his church throughout, his courage or his workmen failed him, and he had to be content with a wooden roof, possibly with alternating transverse arches as at Jumièges and Cérisy. St. Nicholas, Caen, is also Lanfranc's work: here the choir was actually covered by ribless cross vaulting; the triforium is much reduced in importance, as later at the Trinité in Caen and Saint Georges de Boscherville, and finally—after a return to the earlier form — in the standard type of Gothic church, while the architectural treatment of the exterior is still further developed in articulation. Saint Georges de Boscherville is of the same genus and follows after, probably in the very last years of the century or the first of the next.

In spite of the most shocking " restorations " of the end of the nineteenth century which have transformed its interior into a whitewashed and mechanical horror, Saint Georges is — or was — a church of great nobility and finesse of proportion. Its arcade is lofty and fine in form, its triforium low and cut into a level arcade by close-set shafts and narrow arches; the tribunes of the transepts are beautifully designed, while the exterior is admirable in mass and logical and vigorous in detail. The apse was originally vaulted with a simple half-dome, and the choir with plain, unribbed cross vaulting; the present nave vault is of the thirteenth century, but originally it was spanned by great arches, not, as before, on alternating piers, but on all, so forming a stage of development toward the oblong vaulting, as opposed to cross vaulting or sexpartite, of the Gothic church.

It is in England, however, that Lanfranc's greatest works were realized. This is eminently fitting since the successful invasion of England by his duke was due more to him than to anyone else, for it was his brilliant mind and indomitable will and soaring ambition that used the courage of William

as its tool and in the end made of him a
great statesman as well as a daring adven-
turer. To England Lanfranc went, now as
Archbishop of Canterbury, and there, by
the year 1077, he had built a new cathedral,
some portions of which still remain incor-
porated in the vastly extended and many
times rebuilt metropolitan church of England. Lanfranc's work was evidently more
or less a replica of St. Étienne, Caen. St.
Alban's followed immediately, but here
native workmen were apparently used for
the first time, and everything is rude, un-
learned, and primitive: every hint of Lombard craftsmanship and Norman ingenuity
is absent; old materials, Roman and British,
are used over again, and nothing of Norman genius shows itself except in the huge
proportions and the fine directness and simplicity of it all. Lincoln and Winchester
were built at the same time, but little of the
original work is left after the many re-
buildings, except the transept of the latter,
which, though ruder than the work in Normandy, is rich and massive in its pier sections and sets the fashion for the great
abbeys of the succeeding century. The
eleventh century portions of Ely show im-

proved craftsmanship and various interesting minor diversions from the Norman type, amongst them the inclination away from multiple piers toward the great cylindrical shafts of stone later so popular at Durham, Tewkesbury, and Gloucester. It is at the last church, and also at Norwich, that we first find in England the two-story ambulatories around the choir, with a small group of radiating chapels.

The number of great churches built in England between the Conquest and the end of the century was something prodigious, and their dimensions followed suit. The English abbeys of the eleventh and twelfth centuries were the largest structures in Christendom, and fine as they were when first built they never seemed adequate, but were extended, remodelled, and rebuilt for two centuries after a most extraordinary fashion. In their fabulous number and their unheard of dimensions they serve to give some idea of the part played in the Middle Ages by the monks who made them, and of the place religion held then in relation to the people. To these monastic institutions must be added great numbers of cathedrals and parish churches, and as a result we are bound to realize that during this entire period not only was organized religion the chief power in the community and the State, but also that it must have been the intimate and personal interest of every member of society. As a matter of fact the parish was in England the social, and in many ways the political, unit. In the parish councils the lord of the manor was hardly more than one of his tenants. As the chancel belonged to the parson, so the nave was the property of the people, who were bound to keep it in repair and who were as jealous of their duties as they were of their privileges. As Bishop Hobhouse says, "The parish was the community of the township organized for Church purposes, and subject to Church discipline, with a constitution which recognized the rights of the whole body as an aggregate, and the right of every adult member, whether man or woman, to a voice in self government." The roots of liberty and free democratic government, as these have come down to us in theory (though hardly in practice), are to be found far deeper in the old parish of the Mediæval Church than in Parliament or folkthing or shire-mote.

From Apostolic days down to a few centuries ago the Mass was for all Christians a matter of holy obligation, and in every English parish church Mass was said daily, and several times on Sunday. The " Christian year " also, with its unending round of varied festivals and fasts and its commemoration of equally varied saints (to some one of whom each Christian had his own personal devotion), interpenetrated the lives of all the people with an insistence and an individual appeal never equalled before or since. As for the seven Sacraments—Baptism, Confirmation, The Lord's Supper, Matrimony, Penance, Holy Orders, and Extreme Unction — they accompanied everyone from the cradle to the grave, linking each life into the Christian fabric by indissoluble bonds and giving a spiritual significance and sacred character to every event in the life of every man.

The monasteries were never more than a day's journey apart in any direction, and were therefore an ever-present element in life. With the cathedrals they were the great centres of art and beauty in every form, more than adequately taking the place of the art galleries, libraries, opera houses, theatres, and " movies " of the present day, since in them art was alive, operative, and the possession of all. Each had some shrine where precious relics of saints or martyrs were venerated, and the whole country was threaded with pilgrim routes, crowded with devotees who were apparently as jolly as they were devout. These religious houses were the greatest landlords in the realm and their tenants were envied by those who were under secular landlords, since they themselves were more generously treated in every way. Education, mercy, medical science, charity, hospitality, and all the arts were centred in these religious houses, which also acted as trustees and guardians for orphans and minors. They were therefore not only necessarily large to accommodate the monks, lay brothers, scholars, guests, and servants, but often vast because of the enormous part they played in common life and the incredible throngs that came to them for worship and to claim their ministrations.

It is hard for us to think back into such an alien spirit and time as this, and so understand how, with a tenth of its present population, England could have supported so vast and varied a religious establishment, used as we are to an age when religion is only a detail for many, and for most a negligible factor. We are only too familiar with the community that could barely support one parish church, boasting its half-dozen religious organizations, all together claiming the adherence of only a minority of the population, but in the Middle Ages religion was not only the most important and pervasive thing, it was a moral obligation on every man, woman, and child, and rejection, or even indifference, was unthinkable. If we once grasp this fact we can understand how in the eleventh century the whole world should cover itself with its " white robe of churches " and why also their desecrated ruins should so often still manifest the vestiges of the greatest and most universal art the world has ever known.

This work of William of Volpiano and Lanfranc, which we have been considering only too briefly, is of course very rightly called Norman; but I think it a mistake to place it in a category by itself and treat it as an intermediate style that came quite to an end to give place for Gothic as a new and independent creation. Instead of this sequence of quite individual styles there was, I believe, a swift, steady, and logical progress from William of Volpiano's vanished church at Dijon, through Jumièges, Caen, and the English abbeys of the Norman Conquest, to St. Denis, Noyon, Paris, and Chartres, and so to the full flower of Amiens, Coutances, Rheims, York, Westminster. The impulse was one, the goal always the same, but from time to time new influences were brought to bear on the process, and at one definite moment these were so numerous, so potent, and withal so novel that the course of events was not only accelerated but deflected from its original course, the result being the Gothic style. To appreciate these influences we must consider for a moment the twelfth century in its relation to its predecessor and its immediate successors.

The eleventh century burst unheralded on a degenerate and hopeless Europe, but the twelfth was the onward and upward rush of that unparalleled energy already initiated and foreordained to a high destiny hitherto unequalled. The great principle of human association through manageable social units, that after the end of the great

dream of world empire had manifested
itself through Benedictine monasticism and
the feudal system, now extended itself even
more widely and took shape in the parishes,
the village communes, the guilds of traders
and artisans, the great schools and colleges,
and the lay orders of knighthood. Every-
where men came together in brotherhoods,
both secular and religious, and for a century or more Europe was organized on a
socialistic basis which is the only possible
model for similar movements, now or in the
future, and which succeeded just in so far
as it differed from our own contemporary
socialistic schemes, vainly designed to effect
the same ends. The twelfth century was
more truly democratic than any society before or since, if we consider democracy to
consist, not in miscellaneous machinery and
vicissitudinous panaceas, but in certain ends
of right and justice. Today, abandoned as
we are to the frantic invention of the engines and machinery of democracy, and to
the devising of novel and startling nostrums
for the curing of our manifold ills, we have
wholly lost sight of democracy itself and
have even forgotten in what it consists.
Naturally, therefore, it is as hard for us

to comprehend the vital democracy of the Middle Ages as it is to understand the part played by religion in the civilization of the same period. Both, however, are fundamental, and I do not think it possible for anyone either to appreciate or to understand the art of the time without some recognition of them as basic facts.

Perhaps one reason why the democracy of the twelfth century was so successful is that it never failed for leaders, since democracy without high personal leadership is a dead thing that can end only in anarchy, or in that domination by the worst of its elements that finds its nemesis in the inevitable reaction to despotism. The naming of all the great leaders of the time would run to the term of this lecture, and one can do no more than note a few in each category, as for example, amongst the kings, Lothair II, Charles the Fat, Henry Plantagenet, Richard Cœur de Lion, Philip Augustus, Roger of Sicily, with such vivid female personalities as Matilda of Tuscany, Eleanor of Guienne, Blanche of Castile. Amongst the great constructive leaders of thought who were brilliantly forging the wonder of Catholic philosophy were St.

Anselm, St. Bernard, Abelard, William of Champeaux, Peter Lombard, Hugh of St. Victor. In religion we find St. Robert of Molêsme, St. Norbert, St. Thomas à Becket, Peter the Venerable, with, just at the end of the century, the great Pope, Innocent III.

And the following was worthy of the leadership: not only was this, as I have said, the era of the guilds and communes, the great schools and universities, the military orders of knighthood, it was also the age of increasing art in every category: of music, through the trouvères and troubadours, and the *chansons de gestes;* of poetry, through the forming in final shape of the legends of Arthur and of the Holy Grail; of architecture, through the transforming of Norman into Gothic. If ever the *élan vital* rose to inordinate heights of untrammelled creation, it was then; and this vivid vitality seemed to overflow itself in every category of mental and physical and spiritual activity. The development of the system of sacramental or Catholic philosophy is a sufficient exemplar of the first, the career of the Norman adventurers of the second, while the Cistercian reformation is typical of the third. It is only now, in these last days, while our own chosen system of evolutionary philosophy is falling in ruins around us, that we are beginning to think back beyond Herbert Spencer, beyond Kant, beyond Descartes, beyond St. Thomas Aquinas himself, to that very wonderful system that finds perhaps its best exposition in Hugh of St. Victor, and to discover there, in the midst of the twelfth century, a body of illuminating philosophy that is to the Christian world what Plato was to paganism. As for the bodily activity of inordinate adventure, there is nothing more stimulating than the story of the Hautevilles, the eight sons of a poor gentleman of Normandy, five of whom proved themselves conquerors of the first degree, winning in Sicily and southern Italy estates for themselves as well as thrones, now and again, for their descendants. Of course all their compeers were doing the same sort of thing; — conquering England, the Holy Land, even gaining the throne of the Eastern Empire; but the hardy Hautevilles are the best exponent of Norman force, since they show how, in a single family, the ardour of action is not confined to one alone but extends itself through all.

Of the Cistercian reformation I must
speak more at length, since it was the chief
agent in effecting the change from the Norman to the Gothic principle in architecture.
Monasticism, of the type established it
would seem, once for all, by St. Benedict
of Nursia in the sixth century, is an essential element in Christian civilization, re-
curring ever and again when the things
against which it contends have achieved
supremacy and brought society to the point
of ruin. In the sixth, the eleventh, and the
sixteenth centuries it had its most brilliant
manifestations, and already it is preparing
again for its identical office of social regeneration. It is, however, human in its constitution, and subject to the general law of
degeneration, therefore it is constantly laps-
ing from its ideals, its standards, and its
prescribed modes of action. If its work
is not accomplished before this inevitable
retrogression sets in, then another order
comes into existence to continue the labour
under a new impulse of righteousness. The
work of the Middle Ages was not accomplished before the Order of Cluny, that had
made the Normans the most potent forces
in Europe, surrendered to the gravitational

peril of the world, and became rich, self-indulgent, morally lax. By the end of the eleventh century the Benedictines of Cluny had made the art they had re-created a thing of luxury, splendour, and inordinate expense. Cathedrals, abbeys, and churches were vast, massive, elaborate in design, opulent in sculpture and colour and gold. The vestments for the sacred offices, the altar vessels and ornaments, the Mass books and shrines and reliquaries were of a Byzantine luxury in their wealth of gold and silver and precious stones. Art took the place of ethic; ease and luxury and license came in the stead of self-denial, holy poverty, and missionary zeal. Nevertheless the work was only half done; therefore St. Robert of Molesme was moved to a reform that should be a return to Apostolic righteousness and zeal, the Order of Citeaux being the result. It was a glorious return to the Benedictinism of St. Benedict himself, and at once old men and young flocked to the Cistercian monasteries in such numbers that fathers and mothers and wives tried to hide or place under restraint the boys and men of their families in order that they might not yield to the overwhelming call of the cloister. Within a few years of the founding, St. Bernard became a monk of the new order, and then the situation became worse, for now men were neither to hold nor to bind, and secular society was decimated. The result was not, however, what might have been feared by the eugenists of the time (if there were any), for the imposition of the law of celibacy on tens of thousands of the best of both sexes could not depress the standard, and character waxed even finer and more vigorous for several generations.

The effect on architecture was immediate and fundamental: hitherto, with all its magnificence it had been structurally static, a style of inertia. In the Roman basilica the principle of dead loads held practically throughout, for the thrust of the narrow aisle arches was negligible, that of the triumphal arch taken up by the lateral walls of the transept, that of the dome of the apse by its own thick walls. The domical church of the East was indeed active in every part, but with little concentration of thrusts, and the varied and incessant push was met by counteracting masses of inert masonry and walls of enormous thickness. The same

principles held in Normandy and England:
as arches widened in span the walls grew
thicker and more massive, the abutments
more ponderous. With the adoption of
cross vaulting of masonry the resulting concentration of weight and thrusts was ignored
and the intervening wall areas were thick-
ened equally with the local abutments.
Five-foot walls became almost a minimum,
and the thickness was sometimes increased
up to eight or ten feet. Of course the result was the necessity of providing huge
masses of masonry, expensive in themselves
and very tempting to carvers and decorators.
It cannot be denied that these vast and
massive structures have a power and dignity all their own, — as, for example, Peterborough, Ely, Durham, — and they were
so well liked that in England they generally resisted the advent of the new Gothic
fashion of construction, while accepting its
outward forms, and for this reason English
Gothic achieved little of the structural logic
and economy of France. On the whole,
however, the magnificent Norman style was
intolerable to the Cistercian puritans, and
at their instigation the master builders of
the time strove to find a solution that, while

sacrificing nothing of beauty, should yet reduce the initial cost. The success of this effort was triumphant, but it was due to the entrance into the field of a new racial element different alike from the Italianized Lombards of the south and the Christianized Vikings of Normandy. This new element was that of the Franks of the Ile de France, who, under the spur of the Cistercians, brought to bear on the structural problem the acute intellect, the creative ingenuity, and the unfailing logic that were their everlasting contribution to the great and glorious unity we know as the French people. Under their hands architecture was made over, for their quick wit and ready ingenuity soon showed them that by concentrating loads, thrusts, and abutments they could reduce the bulk of their masonry by half, and furthermore, that there were certain physical laws that might be discovered by experiment, if not on *a priori* grounds, and that these laws might be used to determine lines of energy, weights of resistance, and factors of safety. In a word they brought pure science to bear on the question, not as master but as servant, in which respect they differed radically from the devotee of science of today. In time the whole thing turned into a game, and the master builder became obsessed by his science, to the peril of his art as well as of his buildings themselves, but for an hundred and fifty years the just balance was maintained before Beauvais closed the chapter in calamity.

The ribbed and pointed vault had already been worked out, and so had the two forms of sexpartite vaulting, in the abbeys of Caen. The next step was the adoption of the oblong vault area. In the Abbaye des Dames the vault, though comparatively late, is undeniably a survival of the earliest form of high vault, for it is simply a great intersecting vault of equal sides, the transverse crown being reinforced and supported by an arch with its spandrels filled in by a thin wall of stone — manifestly an evidence of doubt on the part of the builders as to the stability of so large a quadripartite vault as is necessary to span a nave always twice the width of the aisle. Incidentally it is also a first step to the oblong area. The vault of the Abbaye aux Hommes is a clumsy approach to the true sexpartite vault, for here the masonry springs back

on either side from the intermediate wall
to meet the main curves of the square
vault, so forming exterior wall surfaces
into which an arched window would accommodate itself without offence. Of
course, as soon as the oblong areas which
naturally followed from the perfected sexpartite form were generally adopted, the
alternating system was given up, and the
regular order of Gothic columniation determined for all time. Simultaneously the
device of stilting was introduced, whereby
sharply pointed arches were avoided and
the full thrust of the vault brought to bear
along a single vertical line above the vault
shafts — a thing as beautiful as it was me-
chanically perfect, for it resulted in that
warping of the vault surfaces which is one
of the most subtle charms of French Gothic
architecture.

The problem of receiving these concentrated thrusts had been partially solved in
Normandy: the old Roman device of huge
masses of masonry, or rather transverse
walls, adopted at Sant' Ambrogio, had been
abandoned, and in his Abbaye aux Hommes
Lanfranc had substituted the half of a barrel
vault running the length of the aisle and

abutting against the nave wall. This was effective but illogical, for only a small part of the buttressing arch received any thrust whatever. Almost immediately, therefore, as in the Abbaye des Dames, the intervening areas were cut away and only the arch at each pier remained. This of course was a true flying buttress, but it was still concealed below the aisle roof, hence the clerestory was restricted in height to the wall area of the vault alone. At Noyon, about the middle of the century, and apparently for the first time, the abutting arch emerged into the open air and the flying buttress with all its possibilities had come into its own.

We have now, you will perceive, nearly all the elements of the Gothic organism: the cruciform plan with wide transepts and deep choir, the vertical order of arcade, triforium and clerestory, pointed arches, ribbed and stilted vaults with oblong compartments, concentrated loads and thrusts, direct abutments, with the flying buttress *in posse,* and the intervening walls reduced by half in thickness; articulation expressed by compound piers and arches, with vault shafts well grounded from vault to floor, lofty proportions, complex compositions of light and shade. All this has worked itself out in the interior of the church; outwardly little change is apparent, for Gothic growth was exclusively from within outward, as it was essentially a logical and an organic growth. We have, it is true, even at Jumièges, the great west towers, with the other over the crossing always favoured in Normandy and therefore in England even to the end of the Middle Ages, but apart from such large and general forms the exterior, even of almost fully developed Gothic structures, still remains, to all intents and purposes, that of a Norman church.

In the meantime the great architectural idea of the chevet, or polygonal apse with its single or double encircling aisle and radiating chapels, forming as it does the great structural and artistic glory of the style, and the point where, intellectually, all the vivid logic of the French master builders shows itself at its highest perfection, had been slowly evolving after a curiously entertaining fashion. When the domical church of Constantinople, Ravenna, and Aix-la-Chapelle was finally superseded by the western and more ancient basilican plan, it was not wholly abandoned, for its possibilities were too great. First of all, the final form of a domed polygon surrounded by a vaulted aisle with shallow projecting bays or apses, was cut in halves and added to the cross-shaped basilica; then it was subjected to the process of concentration, articulation, and scientific refinement that was taking place in the remainder of the fabric, and we obtain the astonishing sequence: a Roman calidarium, Bosrah, Ravenna, Aix-la-Chapelle, St. Martin at Tours, St. Germer de Fly, St. Denis, Chartres, Amiens, and Le Mans. A very interesting evidence of the plausibility of this theory, not, I think, heretofore noted, is the apse of the abbey church at Essen, dated about 1040, which is simply three sides of Charlemagne's chapel at Aix applied to the end of a Romanesque basilican church. We still lack, of course, the Gothic spirit as it showed itself æsthetically, and without this, no matter how highly developed may be our Gothic structural form, we have not the whole of Gothic, for this is a spirit as well as an organic system of building. The effort has been made — as I believe, both unwisely and unsuccessfully — to confine the word " Gothic " exclusively to that work which is perfect in its structural system and its organic form, according to the highest point reached at any time in these directions. This mechanistic and even pedantic method of criticism is of the nineteenth century type of analytical and materialistic mentality, and I doubt if it can maintain itself much longer. Gothic construction is indeed the most highly articulated, the most vividly intelligent, and the most scientifically exact ever devised by man, but it is only a part of Gothic architecture, which is as well the expression of an entirely new social and devotional spirit, engendered by a peculiar, beneficent, and dynamic energy in the world of the west, and expressed through new forms of beauty that have no historic prototypes. The greatest Gothic monuments are such as Chartres and Amiens and Rheims, but all other structures, whether civil or secular, produced between 1150 and 1400 under the influence of Mediæval culture, by the races of the north, are equally Gothic, whether the full structural system is present in all its integrity, or only indifferently, or even not at all.

The sequence of development as recorded

in existing buildings is approximately this: Bury, St. Leu d'Esserent, St. Germer de Fly, St. Denis, after which Gothic is fully, firmly, and finally developed. The space of time involved is from 1125 to 1140, — surely the most astonishing fifteen years in architectural history. In the nave of Bury, begun in 1125, we find the pointed arch used consistently, with ribbed, stilted, and oblong vaults, all handled clumsily and with hesitation, but with undoubted conviction. St. Germer de Fly, begun five years later, is almost as amazing a portent as was Jumièges for its own time, for it was apparently without a prototype, yet here we find all the elements of Bury handled with perfect assurance, and as well a complete articulation of shafting, a chevet very well worked out, the second story gallery reduced to the limits of a true triforium, and all the loftiness of line and grace of proportions that we associate with perfected Gothic. Its flying buttresses are still concealed below the triforium roof, therefore the clerestory is largely blank wall with small pointed windows confined between the spring and the crest of the vaults. Outwardly the church is still sturdily Norman.

Five years later the great Abbot Suger built his fine new Abbey of St. Denis, leaving us, fortunately, a brilliant and enthusiastic account of his aims and his methods. The church was consecrated in 1140; it was immediately followed by Sens, Noyon, Paris, and Laon, and stands, therefore, as marking the point when the vital new tendency reached its fulfilment and Mediævalism achieved its perfect form of expression. Of the original work of Suger only the west front and the ambulatories of the chevet remain, for a century later all the rest of the church was rebuilt in the fully developed Gothic manner, forming one of the great examples of the perfected style. From what remains, however, and from the admirable old abbot's proud narrative, it is evident that at last all sense of hesitation and uncertainty had disappeared; Bury and St. Germer de Fly took their places as the last of the Norman mode in which the spirit of the new Gothic was working hiddenly; St. Denis itself crossed the dividing line and became the first of the great sequence of the monuments of Catholic Christianity that ended only with the advent of the new paganism.

[124]

It was not that any new devices were introduced, for there were none to be discovered; it was rather that the power that was working for self-expression at last acquired its adequate master craftsmen who worked now with confidence and conviction, with a high intelligence irradiated by a kind of divine inspiration, refining and perfecting, articulating and co-ordinating all that a century of devoted and progressive effort had brought to their hands. Now first the Gothic spirit bores itself through from within, outward, the last of the old static Norman is consumed away, and the great progress begins that was to find its apotheosis, just an hundred years later, in the Cathedral of Our Lady of Rheims, destined to stand in all its unapproachable majesty century after century, while the spirit that had created it died away amongst men and the new power in the world worked its will amongst all nations and all peoples; destined at last to be given into the hands of those who best had learned the lesson of this new power and applied its methods, who blasted it with their own consummate engines of destruction and left it shattered, scorched, and desecrated, but with its eternal fabric still intact. Even so, under the same assaults, the everlasting power that brought it into being still stands, shattered, scorched, and desecrated, but, like Rheims, ultimately indestructible, and destined again to redemption and regeneration.

LECTURE V

THE MEDIÆVAL SYNTHESIS

I HAVE tried in the last two lectures to show how, first in Lombardy, then in Normandy, and all within the limits of a century, the essential structural elements of a potential Gothic were being invented or rediscovered, until at last, under Lanfranc, the material was assembled and made ready for that finger-touch of creative vitality that was to transform a casual assembling into coherency, and transfigure it with a new spirit of unexampled power and of beauty unapproachable. In the same way, as I have endeavoured to make clear, an identical process was being followed in civil and ecclesiastical society. Out of equal darkness came equal light, and this new day made possible the artistic transformation that was now to take place. Feudalism had created a new society made up of human units linked by the human bonds of personal attachment and reciprocal duties and privileges. Out of this admirable social scheme came an added impulse toward the ideals of service, obedience, loyalty, honour, chivalry. Monasticism had grown from a protest into a world-wide agency of service, rebuilding the ruined fabric of education and art, creating anew a vast but always human agency of charity, mercy, and hospitality. The guild system, working on from self-protecting alliances of traders, had extended itself to every existing form of industry and commerce, always, as in other domains, of human and manageable scale, until the workman held a position of self-respect and of independence, with an assurance of just and certain compensation, such as he had never held before and has failed to achieve since. In the south, where the lingering tradition of a dead imperialism prevented the normal development of feudalism, the crescent spirit of independence and co-operation made itself visible through the free communes or city-states, where again the basis of association was human in its scale in place of the vast material aggregate of force and military power of the preceding epoch, and of the vague abstractions of political dogmatism,

philosophical theory, and empty shibbo-
leths of that which was to follow.

The ardent and restless spirit of the north
had opened up new lines of pilgrimage and
adventure through Europe, across the Mediterranean, into the mysterious fastnesses of
Africa, Arabia, Syria, the Levant, even into
the frozen north of the heathen tribes, and
the wonder of a doubly mysterious Asia.
The crusades had stirred the spirit of Normandy, Flanders, France, the Rhineland,
England, and opened up new possibilities
of adventure, conquest, treasure, commercial gain, while the paynim principalities
in the south and the decadent empires of
the East were a living incentive to the expanding vigour and the overriding ambition of the uncontrollable races of the north.

With the humanizing of society came an
identical humanizing of religion and of
philosophy. During the patristic days the
Church had been so busy in determining
in exact form the verbal symbols of essential dogma, and in beating down one plausible heresy after another, that the natural
process of devotional development had been
held back, and the latent humanism in the
original deposit of the Faith came but

slowly into view and operation. For five centuries, however, the humanizing process had been going on, and by the opening of the thirteenth century the Church had adapted its system of worship to the eternal and unchangeable demands of the human soul, until it met these at every point. I do not mean to say that anything novel in doctrine was added; it was rather that new spiritual possibilities were revealing themselves through dogmas and practices existing from the beginning, and that new forms of devotion grew up to intensify the appeal of doctrines that dated from the time of the Apostles themselves. For example, the invocation of the saints and prayers for the dead are recorded even in the catacombs and were a part of original Christianity; now, however, the new impulse of human and personal relationship took hold of the ancient doctrines and established a sense of intimate kinship between the individual on the one hand and the hierarchy of angels and archangels, the saints and martyrs, the dead of every family, on the other. This new spiritual intimacy served to bring the divine and the unseen down closer to earth, while lifting man and his common life into closer communion with the whole company of heaven. In the same way the Mass had been, certainly since the post-Apostolic age, both Communion and Sacrifice; now, however, the latter quality was increasingly emphasized and the inevitable corollary of the sacramental presence of Christ in the consecrated species resulted, in the time of Charlemagne, in the clear enunciation of the doctrine of Transubstantiation, though the final definition was not to be determined for many centuries.

An identical process was going on in philosophy, whereby the aloof and abstruse orientalism of the Eastern and Alexandrian schools, and the massive yet precise intellectualism of St. Augustine, were being fused in a comprehensive sacramentalism that was at the same time definitive, since it was an intellectual approximation to an intelligible exposition of the fundamental law of all life, and of unusual appeal through its perfect adaptation to the needs and desires and aspirations of the human soul. This singularly human yet equally exalted philosophy seems to me to find its full flower in Hugh of St. Victor, with St. Anselm and St. Bernard as particular exponents of certain of its more limited aspects.

The dominating influence, then, which determines and emphasizes Mediævalism, is a very real humanism that is in fact the antithesis of that fictitious humanism of the Renaissance which has usurped the name. It moulds and transmits and fixes in definite form every thought and action of the time, and is as fundamental in controlling artistic development as in establishing the nature of the religion, the philosophy, the social system of the Middle Ages. While it resulted in the most perfectly balanced scheme of life that is of record, it was by its very nature peculiarly susceptible of abuse. As the inevitable tendency of mysticism is ever further and further away from the earth into the impalpable ether, until Hugh of St. Victor is merged into St. Bonaventure and so into Hildegarde of Bingen and Fritz Thauler: as the inevitable tendency of pure intellectualism is from St. Thomas Aquinas ever lower and lower through Calvin and Herbert Spencer to the impossible nadir of Haeckel, so the tendency of humanism is toward that disastrous point when all spiritual things are reduced to the level and scale of man himself and there is no longer any distinguishing between the two. Then comes anthropomorphism, the debasing of worship to the level of a series of charms and formulæ, the purchase and sale of sacraments, indulgences, dispensations; the invention of crude and vulgar devotions, with loss, in the end, of spiritual consciousness and even of the very sense of right and wrong.

As a matter of fact, much of all this revealed itself progressively through the latter Middle Ages, and what had been its glory became its shame. As, however, you cannot judge monasticism after the nineteenth century fashion, from its incidents and episodes, and final estate of degradation, but rather by its great epochs when it was in the full flower of its splendour and beneficence, so you cannot judge the Middle Ages from their decadence. What they became after 1305 when the secular power regained control of religion, does not concern us here. The architecture we are considering was the exponent of the culture and civilization of Mediævalism while it was still young and vigorous, or in its majestic maturity. This period lasts, roughly, from the year 1000 to 1300, a space of three centuries, one half of which is the era of youth and endeavour, one half of accomplishment and an only too brief supremacy before the inevitable decline.

I may confess now what you already will have discovered, viz.: that I have undertaken an impossible task in endeavouring to concentrate into six hours not only the art of six centuries but as well something of the spirit and the power that lay behind it. I can now hardly more than refer in the most superficial way to the pregnant events of this amazing time, leaving those of you who are interested, perhaps, to find in Henry Osborne Taylor's " The Mediæval Mind," Dr. Walsh's " The Thirteenth Greatest of Centuries," and Henry Adams's " Mont-Saint-Michel and Chartres," the secret revealed, as in no other books I know, of the dynamic force that took shape in a system of life and thought the perfect expression of which is the art, and especially the architecture, of the central century of the Middle Ages.

Two hundred years of varied monastic influence toward righteousness had at last resulted in a redemption of the Papacy that made it, through the great pontiff, Innocent III, the controlling power in Europe, and Innocent himself a kind of spiritual Lord of the World. All kings were ultimately subject to him, even Philip Augustus of France, whose domestic irregularities wrought an issue between them that was salved only by royal surrender. As Innocent was followed by such worthy successors as Gregory IX and Boniface VIII, so Philip of France was followed by Louis VIII and St. Louis, the last of whom has well been called " the ideal of a loyal knight and a Christian king." And there were great kings in all the world: Frederick Barbarossa, Frederic II, Edward I, Robert Bruce, Rudolph of Hapsburg, Ferdinand III, Alphonso the Wise. Learning and education ascended by leaps and bounds; the universities rapidly made themselves a greater force than the monasteries that had created them, and philosophy, through Albertus Magnus, Duns Scotus, Roger Bacon, Raymond Lully, Alexander Hales, and, greatest of all, perhaps the most supreme intellect of all time, St. Thomas Aquinas, reached a height of almost inconceivable achievement. Arts that had struggled toward the light during the preceding century reached their culmination, and arts long forgotten were born again. The union of music and poetry at the hands of the meistersingers and minnesingers and of those of the creators of the great Latin hymns (the latter a new art altogether) lifted both arts to new and exalted levels, while pure music became perfected in the Gregorian mode. In Siena and Florence painting was reborn in Duccio, Cimabue, and Giotto, while sculpture, restored in France a century before the Pisani in Italy, achieved a fruition that placed it on the same plane as that held by the sculpture of Hellas. So this incredible century proceeds, and at the end all is gathered together in Dante, the eternal synthesis of Mediævalism.

Great as was the thirteenth century in constructive statesmanship, in the fixing of the principles and the laws of civil liberty, in philosophy, and in the development of all the arts (whether the old arts of painting and sculpture and poetry or the new of stained glass, hymnology, illumination), its achievement in architecture was in some ways the most notable, perhaps because what happened there epitomizes all that was done elsewhere, and the nature of what was accomplished is precisely that which informed the whole body of Mediæval achievement.

We have seen how nearly all the structural elements of Gothic already had been brought into being; what remained was the Gothicizing of it all, the giving it essential Gothic quality. This may, I think, be divided under three heads, Cohesion, Economy, and Character. The first means knitting everything together synthetically, giving it a certain dynamic power to grow from within outward in accordance with clear laws and under one impulse, and finally making structure itself, not only efficient as such, but beautiful in itself, the central fact and force in the style, all ornament of every kind being something added, but growing inevitably from it. Economy means the discovery of physical forces, using them in such a way that they work either together or in intelligent and effective opposition, so making possible the reduction of columns, walls, arches, buttresses, vaults, to a logical minimum, but always with regard to that *optical* minimum which prevented a reduction in bulk below a certain point, even if a further diminution would be structurally safe, since the mind must be satisfied, through the eye, and the physical test could not be considered as final. Character is the hardest thing to define, but in a way the most significant. It is the quality that makes a thing Gothic whether its structural system is of the perfectly developed type or not. It is what the glass of Chartres, the sculpture of Amiens, the pictures of Giotto, the Hora Novissima, the High History of the Holy Grail, all possess in common with the great cathedrals, and in so full a degree that they may all be called Gothic, or Mediæval, or if you like Catholic. Singly and together they are the creation and the expression of the one epoch when Catholicism interpenetrated all life to such an extent that no single portion of society except the Jews, the Mohammedans, and the as yet unconverted tribes of Prussia, were outside its scope or beyond its influence and control. Character means for us difference in quality, and this is both material and spiritual. Saint Georges de Boscherville has, for example, almost as many Gothic elements in its construction as the Cathedral of Sens, but the one is essentially Norman in character, the other just as essentially Gothic. The character of the mouldings in Cérisy is of one type, that of Noyon absolutely different, and the same is true of the scheme, the material, and the detail of design. The ornament of the later Norman and Romanesque is rich and elaborate beyond Gothic comparison, until the fifteenth century, but it differs as completely from that of Chartres or Amiens or Lincoln as it does, on the other hand, from that of Greece. The placing of ornament, also, is wholly different, and a new theory of composition grows out of a new energy.

What is it that determined all this, and in thirty years gave to architecture a new character that it retained for nearly three centuries? It is, I think, that sudden achievement, by certain peoples, of their majority. Into the golden chalice of life are poured, from a score of flagons, the streams of living water; little by little the chalice brims higher and higher, and at last — at one moment it is full but continent, at the next it overflows. Blood of the North, religious fervour and devotion, a new and fine economic system, a stimulating philosophy, liberal education, personal freedom, sense of honour, chivalry, service, all assemble to the filling of the cup, and between 1150 and 1175 it brims to the full, runs over, and a new stylistic epoch in architecture is accomplished.

Behind and through it all is the new humanism. Our Lady and the saints are friends and defenders, and their service is the pleasure and the duty of chivalry. The world is seen to be very beautiful, with its flowers and its birds and kind little beasts of the woods. Personal allegiance and friendship, and an almost mystical reverence for women bind all kinds and classes with close bonds. Men are free, and as freemen, brave and laborious: the guilds make all work honourable and give each man his chance of self-expression and emulation. All environment is beautiful, all costumes full of life and colour, men are imbued with the beauty and the splendour of religious and secular ceremonial, ugly things disappear and more and more lovely things take their place. Unconsciously men have come to like good things and to make only good things, and the race — not the patron, the amateur, or the isolated artist, — expresses its own and intimate self.

In the last lecture I came with you down to that final quarter of the twelfth century where at St. Denis and Sens, Gothic architecture had shown itself in all its potential force: from them we go straight to Notre Dame in Paris; for here, working from east to west, we can see the process of complete development.

The great church was begun in 1163, only twenty years after St. Denis, the choir of course coming first, and the work gradually extending itself westward until the façade with its towers was finished in its present state in 1235. The plan is fine, clear, and well articulated, but the vertical order is and always was defective. It follows the Norman Abbaye aux Hommes and has a lofty vaulted gallery in place of the low triforium of the Abbaye des Dames, and is in this sense inferior to the somewhat earlier Sens where the triforium is of very great beauty. In Notre Dame, again, cylindrical columns are used for the nave arcade throughout, the vaulting shafts resting on their caps. I have never understood why this device — a distinct retrogression in point of articulation — should be so much admired by critics. At Sens this stopping off the vault shafts occurs only on the intermediate columns, which is admirable, since there the scheme is alternating and the vault sexpartite, the piers carrying the transverse ribs, and therefore the major part of the weight, perfectly expressing their function by being divided into five colonettes, each of which takes a member of the group of vault ribs, grounding them all solidly at the pavement. The perfect system is of course that at Chartres, and almost invariable thereafter, i.e. a smaller circular shaft with four attached colonettes, one reaching from floor to vault and carrying the transverse rib, one performing the same function in the aisle, with those on either side taking the inner ring of the moulded arches of the arcade. The colonettes that take the diagonal ribs of the high vault are either stopped on the top of the arcade cap, or better still at the base course of the triforium, while the longitudinal ribs find their support at the clerestory level.

The nave must have been finished about 1196, and in 1210 the west front was begun and completed in fifteen years. About 1230 there was a serious conflagration, and at that time the novel but unbeautiful round windows above the triforium in each bay were cut out to allow the lengthening of the clerestory windows, and at the same time the original and fine scheme of double buttressing in the chevet was abandoned for the irrational and inorganic flying buttresses leaping both aisles, and grieving the logician as much as they excite the admiration of the tourist. These same preposterous buttresses are one of the first evidences of the inevitable danger that lurked in the scientific proficiency of the French, who were always trying for some new structural wonder and only desisted when Beauvais, which they had pushed even beyond the limits of reason, collapsed in ruin, and, after an humiliating bolstering up by additional supports, remained a vast fragment as the monument to overriding ambition. Impossible as they are, these buttresses, or rather these buttress pinnacles, are examples of the most exquisite detail to be found in the style, and here again we find a premonition of the fate in store when the integrity of construction was lost and Gothic became the riot of marvellous decoration that is called Flamboyant.

Between 1245 and 1250 the nave chapels between the buttresses were constructed — another serious error in judgment — and the transepts were pushed outward a bay, while at the very end of the century the apsidal chapels were built, the ambulatory originally having no chapels whatever. Notre Dame stands as a living record, therefore, of all stages of Gothic during its first period, but no portion can match the west front which marks the culmination of the style. It is perhaps the noblest architectural conception of man, classical in its simplicity, its matchless proportions, the brilliancy of its design, the perfect scale of its detail, the subtle rhythm of its delicate variations.

Amongst the other great cathedrals essentially of the twelfth century we find Noyon, Laon, Senlis, Poitiers, Bourges, and Chartres. It is impossible to describe them now, for each deserves a lecture by itself. Infinite in their variety, they are all under the same inspiration. Laon has its perfectly proportioned plan and its great scheme of seven clustering spires; Soissons has its

wonderful south transept which Porter
calls "one of the most ethereal of all
twelfth century designs and the highest expression of that fairy-like, Saracenic phase
of Gothic art that had first come into being
at Noyon." As for Bourges, it is unique,
and to me the finest Gothic interior in the
world, with its vast, transeptless nave, its
five aisles, and its pyramidal system of arch-
ing that lifts the nave arcade half as high
again in proportion as in any other church,
its glimmering forest of shafts vanishing
above in luminous shadow. Chartres of
course remains in the end the noblest work
of Gothic art, even though almost every
other church excels it in some single point.
In spite of the bewigged canons of the
eighteenth century who desecrated its choir
with cheap imitation marbles and its sanctuary with a riotous high-altar that looks
like a Broadway burlesque, and then
smashed some of the matchless windows in
order that the world might see the results
of their stupendous crime — in spite of this
Chartres remains less wrecked within by
bigotry, revolution, the vulgarity of the
eighteenth and the restorations of the nineteenth century, than any other of the great

cathedrals, and it still retains the vast majority of its original glass, which is to this art what the west front of Notre Dame is to architecture — its final, perfect, and divinely inspired word. Add to this blazing vesture of apocalyptic splendour the south tower of the west front, an unparalleled model of serene design, inscrutable proportions, and just composition; the porches of the transepts, which have no prototypes, no rivals, no possible successors, but stand as the revelation through some unknown master-masons of all that is final in inspired design, and finally the sculpture, west, north, south, which leaves no further word to be said in the sensitive adaptation of this art to architecture, — combine all these and add a certain poignant spiritual aroma of the chanted worship and the old incense and the ascended prayers of seven centuries, and you have a thing that almost transcends experience and can only be analyzed by Huysmans, only put into burning words by so consummate a lover and artist as Henry Adams.

The thirteenth century goes on from Bourges and Chartres without a break to Coutances, Amiens, and Rheims. It goes on to innumerable other masterpieces as well, in England, Flanders, Spain, for despite the many small nationalities, perhaps because of them, Europe was practically an unity, fashioned, expressed, and made active through diversity. In France, however, perfection was most closely approached, and national, individual, stimulating as they are, the Gothic monuments of all these peoples never quite approached Chartres, Bourges, Coutances, Amiens, and Rheims in perfect organism, in perfect beauty, and in the indissoluble union of the two. In these masterpieces the progress of development from the simple to the complex, from the almost rudimentary norm of the Athenian temple, each portion of which was perfected to finality, on to the Catholic cathedral of the thirteenth century, where the norm is in itself complex and each detail raised almost to the level of Hellenic perfection, is steady and unbroken, and at Rheims we could see, only two years ago, the triumph of final achievement.

Coutances is not French Gothic, it is Norman Gothic, just as the same art in England — barring Westminster — is Norman by descent. There is a great difference

in this, and one that always should be regarded, for it marks a great divergence and
lessens the contrast so often drawn between,
for example, Lincoln and Bourges. Coutances has the might and majesty of the
work of Lanfranc, with the central tower
so typically Norman and English. On the
other hand its verticality is stupendous: it
soars into the air with a swiftness and clarity
of line almost without equal. The French
cathedral does not do this: there is in it
nothing ponderous, nothing earth-bound,
but it seems to rise with a certain self-
controlled majesty, expressing only its
splendid logic and its magisterial calm.
Coutances is like a troop of lifting spears,
light, strong, exultant, and its effect comes
from conscious design in form, not through
wealth of fretted ornament, for of this there
is little enough. As the chief monument
of Norman Gothic it is a church that well
deserves to be better known than it is.

It is as hard to speak of Rheims as of the
loved and newly dead. For every architect
it had come to be the epitome of his art,
the Parthenon of Christian architecture.
For every friend of France, every devotee
at the shrine of immortal history, it stood

as a radiant apotheosis. For those who still hold by Christianity it was a holy place, with a dim yet penetrating sanctity that silently conquered all doubt, all denial, all derision. There was none other quite like it; not St. Peter's, nor Hagia Sophia; not even Westminster. The insolence of heresy, the brutishness of revolution, the smug self-complacency of restoration had stripped it of its altars, its shrines, its tombs of unnumbered kings, but even the destroyers had venerated its lofty majesty and respected its integrity, while the wars of six centuries had swept around its unscathed walls, impotent for evil in the light of its stainless glory.

For two years it has lain under the fitful storming of shell and shrapnel, doomed to slow death because it is the crowning symbol of a great culture that is an offence to modernism in arms, and of a spirit in man and over man that may not be allowed to exist in the same world with its potent negation. The glass that rivalled Chartres is splintered in starry dust on the blood-stained pavement and its fragments made the settings in soldiers' rings. Its vault is burst asunder by bombs, its interior calcined by conflagration, the incredible sculptures of its portals blasted and burned away. Yet it stands in its infinite majesty, gaunt and scathed in a circle of ruin, still the majestic fabric of a great people, a great epoch, a consummate art.

It was the crowning monument, in material form, of Christian civilization; so perfect in all its parts that it was perhaps too perfect, as being more than man should be permitted to attain, an infringement on the creative power of God. Beyond this was nothing greater, and in Amiens, which is chronologically but a few years younger, we already begin to feel the working of that pride of life and vainglory of conscious competence that forebodes the beginning of the decline.

To most travellers, I suppose, Amiens is the most beautiful cathedral in France, the perfection of fully developed Gothic. Certainly its towering interior, taller in proportion to its width than anything yet accomplished, is awe-inspiring; its sculptures quite by themselves in their vivacity, their masterly design, and their subtle delicacy of execution. The west front, wholly without stylistic consistency and dating from

many periods, is lyric poetry done into
stone. There is no other Gothic front
quite like this in its pictorial composition,
its wealth of intricate design (as rich
as the masterpieces of the Flamboyant
period without their lace-like texture and
their irrational fantasticism), its marvellous
carved ornament which is undeniably the
most varied, original, and exquisite of any
church in the world. In spite of this
there is something lacking, or rather something added that should not be there. Very
hiddenly, very unwholesomely, human
pride is asserting itself above the solemn
devotion of Chartres, the serene Christian
confidence of Rheims. Logic is winning
the mastery, structural engineering is eating
into architectural integrity. Higher and
more tenuous the slim shafts lift themselves
from the pavement: in the marvellous
chevet stone is pared away until the thin
masonry is like a perilous scaffolding:
every foot of wall between buttresses gives
place to the airy tracery of great windows,
and the vault itself soars in the air as though
held down by the taut pull of the colonettes
instead of resting on them as on its natural supports. Of course the painted glass

is nearly all gone, if it ever existed, and the vast interior, whitened by lamentable restorations, is a dizzy blaze of intolerable light. Were these crystal walls glowing with the transcendental splendour of Chartres, or with the glory that was Rheims, our judgment might be different, for then Amiens would be the fulfilment of the dream of its daring creators, where now it is little more than the white ashes of burnt out fires. So great is the part played in Mediæval architecture by this art of glass, created then out of nothing to add a new joy to life, a new wonder to the body of universal art. No church where sacrilege has extinguished this flame of life — and they are the vast majority in every land — should be judged as it stands any more than you would venture to estimate the value of the Brahms Requiem from an orchestral performance from which the voices of the soloists and chorus were excluded, or the Fifth Symphony without the violins. With our taste hopelessly debased by the catastrophic products of glass-makers in the nineteenth century, we naturally cannot understand the part played of old by this triumphant art, unless we have seen for ourselves the miracle of Chartres with its glass so providentially preserved.

In any case, however, the lurking peril was there; not salient, not vociferous enough to injure its perfection, not sufficiently visible to serve even as a warning, but the next stage was the chevet of Le Mans, and the final stage was Beauvais, and through these we can trace the first evidences of decadence back to Amiens, still serene in its perfect mastery.

I have left myself scant space, indeed I have left no space at all, to deal with the other racial and national expressions of Mediæval culture through the varied versions of what was yet one definite Gothic style. This is unjust to Spain and Portugal, where a divergent Gothic showed itself early and ended at last in the fantastic and riotous fancies of Burgos and Poblet. It is unjust to western Germany and Austria, where, though late, a Teutonic version of French Gothic produced a few really national masterpieces. It is unjust to Italy, for though the true Gothic, such as the ruined abbeys of Casamari and San Galgano, are merely Cistercian importations from Burgundy, the friars' churches of the sculptor Arnolfo not Gothic at all and very ugly at that, and the pictorial façades of Orvieto and Siena merely delightful essays in arbitrary design, there *is* a real Mediæval expression in the unique churches of Sicily, with their mingling of Byzantine, Arab, and Norman genius, and in the developed Lombard of North Italy at Pisa, Lucca, Prato, Pistoja. It is doubly unjust to England, for there we find a school of undoubted Gothic which is quite unlike that of France, yet in spirit the same. The divergence is very complete. As I said before, English Gothic inherits directly from Normandy, not from France, and is therefore always more static, massive, and structurally conservative. Moreover there is a fundamental difference in genus due to the same difference in the people. As opposed to the French with their clear logic, which is sometimes almost cruel, the English are incorrigible sentimentalists, always thinking things are better than they are, and that they can easily make them better still by impulsive and almost unpremeditated action. Apparently we, ourselves, inherit directly from them and are therefore hopelessly addicted to the worship of abstract ideals which do not exist and would not work if they did, while our incorrigible optimism prevents our ever seeing a danger (if it is clearly indicated for the future), or of recognizing its advent until the time for preventive action is past and nothing is possible but the desperate struggle for life.

So in England we find, in her Mediæval architecture, a curious clinging to established precedents, a shrinking from novelties in structural development, a more or less complete carelessness of logic, a doing of things because they like them that way and not because it is necessarily the reasonable thing to do. And yet, combined with this is always a curious and very appealing struggle toward the symbolical expression of things almost too high for expression. As the Norman abbeys are vaster, more dramatic, and more overpowering than their prototypes, with their massive construction, their cavernous portals, their giant piers, as at Gloucester, almost Egyptian in their proportions, so with Gothic, when it became the universal mode of expression. Vast towers lift themselves at the west and over the crossing; lancet windows prolong themselves upward to improbable heights; new and irrational compositions are tried as in the astonishing west portals of Peterborough, while the plan pulls itself out to inordinate lengths, and doubled transepts and great chapels prolong the awe-inspiring vistas, and add space beyond space to the blue mystery of nave and choir and aisles. It is all very appealing, particularly to us who are of the same blood and temper, but it offers a tempting opportunity to the mechanistic mind that thinks only in terms of logic, law, and clean-cut definitions.

Of course it is true that we must judge English Gothic by what is left, and this not always of the best. What Henry VIII could not destroy was sacked and wrecked by the Puritan reformers, and what they left the nineteenth century pounced upon as prey for the " restorations " of Wyatt, Lord Grimthorpe, and Sir Gilbert Scott. Salisbury remains, with all its defects upon its head, but Guisborough is gone; of the great northern abbeys only fragments exist, and St. Mary's Abbey, at York, which must have been the most perfect Gothic in England, after having stood roofless and crumbling for three centuries, yielded in the era of enlightenment, which is to say, the early nineteenth century, to the cupidity of commercialism, and was pulled down and burned into lime.

Some faint idea of the ruthless destruction of the noblest art that was carried on under the direction of the " Defender of the Faith " may be gained from Abbot (now Cardinal) Gasquet's " Henry VIII and the English Monasteries," but it is well to have in mind that the nineteenth century was even more ignorant and rapacious than the sixteenth, though its devastations were carried on with less violence, albeit with equal effectiveness.

LECTURE VI

THE DECADENCE AND THE NEW PAGANISM

I HAVE called this last of my lectures
" The Decadence and the New Paganism,"
but the title is incorrect as applied to all that
immediately followed the crest of a great
art as it manifested itself in Amiens, Lincoln, and Rheims. For a long time to come
it was to be a great art, gaining at one place
what it lost at another, and in England los-
ing nothing, but proceeding always on its
serene way until it produced the first truly
national style, that was still at its perfection
when suddenly cut off by the Reformation.
In society, however, the decadence was very
real, and its inception almost immediate.
When, in 1270, St. Louis, " the very perfect
king in Christiantie," went to his eternal
reward, the climax had been reached, more
man could not achieve than already had
been won, and, as always in history, the
curve began to decline.

Art did not follow this swift declension, for it never does. While it is true that art is engendered only by the power of a great ardour and a great righteousness in society, the impulse lasts long after the initial energy is spent. The wave that first shows itself in a low, long swell far out at sea, rising as it advances, and cresting on the edge of the shingle, to burst, fall, and disperse in shallow ripples, only to be sucked back into the abysses of the sea, casts, in falling, its wind-blown foam far forward, until it touches the very grasses of the shore. So with each epoch of civilization and its art; the curve of one is of longer radius, and tangent to the other, continuing, before its inevitable fall, long after the primal impulse has ceased to act. This is why we always find the highest achievements of any art synchronizing with that low level of ethics, of philosophy, of religion, of conduct that follows the epochs of noblest culture and most vivid and wholesome life.

After St. Louis and St. Thomas, after Rheims and Dante, the curve was bound to decline. Already a very unpleasant form of heresy had raised its head in the south of France; the Crusades had degenerated into marauding expeditions, and in the very first years of the fourteenth century the French crown had seized upon the Papacy, establishing over it the secular control Hildebrand had died to avert. " The exile at Avignon " followed, with one after another of the French agents acting as pontiff, and in its trail came the " Great Schism "; a full century, in which secular control of the Church demonstrated all the loss of spiritual independence, all the paralyzing of the power of the Church in the defence of faith and morals, that is its inevitable corollary. Abandoned by its secular and spiritual sovereigns Italy lapsed at once into anarchy and an encroaching barbarism: in Germany the Empire broke down and a new and vicious form of feudalism took its place: the Hundred Years' War devastated France and debauched the moral sense of England, while the Black Death swept Europe like a pestilential flood. Rebellion broke out against the ordered government of the European states, and once more the waves of invasion threatened the almost undefended frontiers, this time in the shape of Turks and Tartars. The Latin Kingdom of Jerusalem fell, the fragments of the

Eastern Empire shrunk smaller and closer under the endless assaults of Bulgars and Turks, although in Spain the tide had turned and Ferdinand III was steadily crushing back the Moslems that at one time had threatened all Europe.

It was a time of terrible choice, of critical peril, but as yet the day was not necessarily lost. A Philip Augustus, an Otto III, an Anselm, a Thomas à Becket, a Leo IX, a Hildebrand, might have met the crisis and theoretically at least have saved civilization. Italy alone had definitely apostatized from its Mediæval ideals, Germany and France were but in the first stages of infection, while England was as yet wholly immune and Spain vigorous with strong new life. A firm hand in the Papacy, righteous kings in France and Germany, a new Cluny or a new Citeaux, might have saved the day. Instead Philip the Fair comes to blight all St. Louis had brought into flower; the earlier Hapsburgs could not avert the nemesis of Germanic order prepared by the last of the Hohenstaufens. The Mendicant Orders, in spite of the best intentions in the world, formed but dissolving bulwarks against a tide that had broken helplessly before the inviolable ramparts of Benedictinism, whatever its special form or name. Inch by inch the virus engendered in Italy during the time of its abandonment by the Popes crept through the veins of Europe. Northward it advanced without stay on that progress that was not to cease until at last, two hundred years later, it was to achieve during the tyranny of the regents of Edward VI final supremacy over England, the last stronghold of Christian civilization.

All this was happening darkly underneath, on the surface was a brave show of culture and refinement. Chivalry was flaunting its splendid pageantry from sea to sea, and almost every year was born some child who later was to be the voicing of a great civilization only the dregs of which remained to him. Nearly all the great painters of Christendom were born in that century that reached from the beginning of the " Great Schism " to the election of the Borgia — Alexander VI. With them came the Blessed Jeanne d'Arc, Savonarola, Erasmus, Sir Thomas More, Bayard, St. Ignatius Loyola, St. Philip Neri ; but simultaneously those whose destiny it was to play each his part in bringing a great epoch to an end in ignorance, anarchy, and apostasy: Machiavelli, Luther, Cranmer, Thomas Cromwell, Henry VIII, and the spawn of the house of Borgia.

It was a field of Armageddon; the armies were drawing together, all the hosts of Heaven waited expectant, and in the year 1453 the great battle began. Constantinople fell before the devouring Turks, and over Italy poured the flood of decadent philosophy, evil morals, and false learning that had festered there during the last years of Byzantine corruption. It came in specious and engaging guise: the spirit of the early Renaissance (which was really Christian and beneficent in so many ways) seized upon it with avidity, wolfed it down, good and evil alike, and was transmuted into a thing profligate, atheist, anarchical. Nicholas V and Pius II tried too late to stem the tide and turn it into the channel of compromise. They were followed by an Alexander VI, a Julius II, and a Leo X. Savonarola, fighting almost single-handed against the hell-let-loose in Italy, went to his martyrdom. Cardinal Cusa, St. John Capistran, and Erasmus were swept before the whirlwind unleashed by Luther and Zwingli. Calvin,

Beza, and the Huguenots, acting in bloody concert with Marie de Medicis and a Catholicism now almost wholly debauched by Italy, turned France into a shambles. The temporal victory remained with the Catholics, but it was empty of righteousness and, unchecked, the Renaissance went on its course. At last the cliffs of England, that had so long withstood the rising tide, yielded to its assault, and Henry, Cromwell, and Cranmer rose to triumph over Sir Thomas More, Bishop Fisher, and the martyrs of monasticism. The exile at Avignon had borne its fruit and Catholic civilization had come to an end. What followed was new: whether for good or ill is not to be considered now, but it was in no sense Catholic, and, whether for good or ill, the Middle Ages were Catholic, first, last, and always.

There was little enough of all this in the architecture that followed immediately on Amiens and Rheims. Beyond their organic perfection there is no further field for development, except along the lines of engineering, and this becomes ever more brilliant and more daring. The chevet of Le Mans is a degree beyond that of Amiens in its delicacy, its complicated articulation, and its beauty; a magical web of stone. Beauvais passes the perilous edge, and as even today, in the heyday of efficiency and consummate engineering, the bridges of able experts will fall now and then, so in France experience rose superior to logic and mechanism and made them of no avail. Beauvais was taller than Amiens, more attenuated than Le Mans, and twelve years after it was finished it crumbled and fell into its own nave. Rebuilt, with humiliatingly necessary reinforcements, it acquired new transepts that were finished in 1550, and a central spire nearly 450 feet high. Again ruin overtook it; the incredible spire fell and was never again rebuilt, while the nave had never even been begun; so the cathedral remains a monument of the decadence; truncated, patched up, semi-ruinous, as Paris stands for the crescent years of Mediævalism, Rheims for its culmination.

Beauvais is sheer beauty, unalloyed, and therein lay its weakness. Its choir, as you first see it, towering above the huddled houses below, is so marvellous that you catch your breath in awe and admiration. It is not wire-drawn and frail like Le Mans,

but composed of solid and almost unornamented buttresses, lifting dizzily into the
air, and thin lace-like arcs springing one
above the other toward the crystal walls of
the clerestory. No finer conception exists,
and no more brilliant and poetic design.
As for the transepts, which were not begun
until the first years of the sixteenth century,
they are of the last Gothic of France at its
best, and this best was good indeed if you
consider it as pure decoration. Where this
new style, called Flamboyant, came from,
and why, is one of the architectural mys-
teries. The balanced art of Amiens continued along established lines for a generation, then froze slowly into a respectable
formalism that ceased suddenly when the
civilization that had created it perished for
the time being in war and desolation. For
almost a century art of every kind was in-
operative, and when it began again it was
on sudden and novel and, it must be con-
fessed, very captivating lines.

When St. Louis died, he left France rich,
powerful, happy. He himself had become
the most dominant prince in Christendom,
and there seemed no reason why his people
should not enjoy in peace, for generations,

the fruit of his noble and knightly labours.
Less than seventy years after his death, and
just a century after the consecration of
Rheims, the " Hundred Years' War " broke
out, and under the unrighteous scourging
of the English king, France was wrecked,
pillaged, devastated, and reduced to the
lowest levels of misery and humiliation.
All the north and east were swept by a
whirlwind of destruction almost like that
which has come on Flanders and Cham-
pagne during these latter years, only then
the cathedrals and abbeys and churches
stood inviolate, rising in the purity of their
new white stone. alone in the abomination
of desolation.

By the year 1270 architecture had become
largely stereotyped along fine but mechanical lines, St. Ouen, Rouen, serving as a
good example, and no great original works
were attempted except Limoges, Narbonne,
and Alby. With the English war work
stopped altogether, and yet, after a space
of sixty years, and at the very moment of
the deepest humiliation of France, suddenly, somehow, came the flush of a new
art, as though to signalize the birth of the
girl who was to listen, alone amongst the

people of her race, to the mystical Voices, and, at the head of a regenerated army, lead her king to his crowning in Rheims, and redeem France. The Blessed Joan of Arc was born in 1411, and seven years later Notre Dame de l'Epine was begun, the first considerable example of the wonderful new art that seemed to grow out of death and corruption, as though men were sick from inordinate misery and turned to beauty, as they were turning back to religion, to find there their only consolation. Caudebec followed in 1426, St. Maclou in 1432, the transepts of Beauvais in 1500 and the church at Brou in 1505. It was a century of the most exuberant worship of beauty: hardly a church in France lacks some embellishment of this period, for the coming of peace in 1456 found a chastened people, who set to work to express their new liberty and their gratitude in the old and honourable way.

Some say the artistic stimulus came from Flanders, some even from England, which in this instance deserved so little either of gratitude or of imitation, but it seems to me that there was material enough already in France. What was done was the isola-

[168]

tion of the decorative and artistic forms
from their structural context, and the transforming of these into a magnificent and
ingenious scheme of ornamentation. So
considered it offers little opportunity for
adverse criticism. It is a wonderful complex of exquisite lines, supple, and flowing:
of crisp, close-set carving, of buttresses that
have been transformed into fretted spires,
of spires that become lace-like canopies, of
canopies that toss themselves like spray into
the air. In spite of its riotous abundance,
its whimsical fancy, its overwrought sentiment, it is always in good taste in France,
and usually in Flanders, though in Spain
and Portugal it rapidly became turgid and
ugly, while in Germany it ended by being
ridiculous.

From the first it grew steadily better in
France, and often reached heights of positive greatness, as in the Tour de Beurre of
Rouen, and in Malines cathedral. Notre
Dame at Louviers, St. Maclou at Rouen,
and Alençon are toys, but St. Germain at
Amiens is a consistent and admirable little
church, as are many others of the same kind.
throughout the country. In almost every
case, however, the beauty is external: within

the work is dry, thin, often ugly in proportion, which is evidence of the great change that has taken place in motive. Secularism is dominant, wealth and luxury increasing, and for the first time outside show takes precedence of the worship of God. Beauty is now sought for its own sake, not as divine service, and the end is not far away. " Art for art's sake " will serve for a time and produce the show of æsthetic competence, but it is impermanent as a motive force and its ultimate degeneration and extinction are not to be escaped.

In England the last phase of Christian architecture was the exact antithesis of that on the Continent. We already have seen that the English Gothic was based on Norman rather than on French foundations and therefore static and conservative; curiously enough it is emotional, as opposed to the clear logic, the nervous energy of development, and the intellectualism of France. It passed through many phases from the Norman William of Sens to the ultra-English William of Wykeham, striking out conceptions of wonderful beauty, such as Netley Abbey and St. Mary's, York, the eastern transepts of Durham and Fountains, Lin-

coln choir and presbytery, Guisborough,
Exeter, Beverly. It devised those wide,
low compositions that are the charm of
English cathedral landscape; it created
towers of singular grace and nobility, and
west fronts of varied and novel majesty.
It invented and perfected the vaulted chapter house and made the abbey and the country church models of almost faultless design.
It turned the simple and little-varied profiles of mouldings, and the somewhat stereotyped pier and arch sections, of France and
Normandy, into living forms of infinite
vitality and variety, and in its carved decoration it has no rival. It is true Gothic of
a very personal and national character, but
it is not the greatest Gothic because it is
undeveloped in its structural organism.

At the very moment when French Gothic
had hardened into a series of formulæ, that
is to say, the first quarter of the fourteenth
century, English Gothic took up an entirely
new line of development that was to give it
a fresh but evanescent glory. It began as
a scheme of decoration, with the remodel-
ling of the choirs of Gloucester and Canterbury, and of the Norman Winchester from
end to end. All this work is practically

contemporaneous and runs from about 1350 to 1400. It is quite unstructural and consists chiefly in a sheathing of thin stone, where all the lines are predominantly vertical, very numerous, and delicate to a degree in their profiles and sections. The revolt from the massive forms and strong, rich lights and shadows of the earlier work is startling. New forms of arch are devised — three-centred, four-centred, elliptical, segmental — and the vaulting, which already had been marvellously enriched, as at Exeter, with many intermediate ribs, took on new shapes, on curious circular or curved section lines, until it came to be known as fan vaulting. Geometrical tracery gave place to many vertical bars, with cross mullions, and ingenious new line-combinations for the heads, while ornament swerved from the exquisitely naturalistic forms of the thirteenth century and became conventionalized and heraldic.

If we were to judge this nascent style from its earliest efforts we should be forced to condemn it as a piece of unstructural artificiality, but no sooner had it made itself fashionable, which it did at once and most inordinately, than a curious thing happened.

Beginning as a scheme of surface decoration, it proceeded to change its whole nature and become logically structural, and so, at last, England actually acquired a form of architectural expression which was not only quite original, but more consistent, as an organic scheme, than anything that had gone before. At once the old and almost cumbersome bulk of the Gothicized Norman gave place to the nervous and completely articulated system of Perpendicular. Columns became slim and widely spaced, walls were thinned to curtains and then to mere veils of glass in a slender scaffolding of stone mullions. The angular and ugly crisscrossing of irrational ribs that had defaced the vaulting of the latest Decorated and the earliest Perpendicular work, disappeared, and fan vaulting, delicately panelled, and split into thin severies by sheaves of slim ribs, took its place. The rich and sonorous glass of the thirteenth century gave place to pale and opalescent compositions of the most delicate yet vivid colour, and this bright adornment spread itself over shafts and walls and vault until the whole interior became a jewel-box of colour and beaten gold.

It was the gayest of all gay styles, flaunting all the glittering pageantry of chivalry, and expressing in perfect form the luxury and the ease and the pride of life that just preceded the Reformation. A great style, though narrow in its scope and secular rather than religious, it imposed itself on England to such a degree that it became the only possible style, and it produced not alone such positive works of genius as the cloister of Gloucester and its Lady Chapel, the vaults of Oxford Cathedral and Sherborne, King's College Chapel and that of Henry VII at Westminster, but as well a bewildering galaxy of town and country churches. England was growing rich and full of plenty: her people were still free citizens, there was as yet no proletariat and no capitalism, the monasteries had not been suppressed, and in spite of the Wars of the Roses and the Black Death, there was greater wealth, more justly distributed, than anywhere else in the world. It was "Merrie England" in truth, and the general content and prosperity showed themselves in an incredible amount of building, both religious and secular, and the embellishing of the old sanctuaries with a fabulous wealth of altars, chantries, screens, tombs, chapels, porches, sculptures, and decorations. It is a pity so little of all this exquisite embellishment has remained. Within a century the major part was beaten into dust, melted into bullion, or sold for building-stones and old metal by the dull-witted and rapacious servants of Henry VIII; and later came "the tiger's cub" Edward VI, Elizabeth, the Puritans, and the nineteenth century. We are thankful for what we have, but its strange beauty makes us hopelessly covetous of the inestimable treasures we have lost.

Toward the end architecture itself hardened a little and lost its spontaneous gaiety and its delicate fancifulness, but in domestic building and in the country churches it continued to the very end. Abbot Huby's fine tower at Fountains had only just been finished when the vast abbey was handed over to pillage and destruction, and the same is true of the lost Edgar Chapel at Glastonbury. Prior Moon's great tower at Bolton had only risen a third of its height at the Suppression, and I myself have found at Fairford the patterns on the unfinished stone, stencilled there by some sixteenth century apprentice in preparation for the master carver who was to come the next day to begin his carving. He did not come, nor ever will, though four centuries have passed since word came that the spoilers were on their way and that no more might be done for the glory of God or for sheer joy in the doing of beautiful things.

Gothic art did not die of inanition. When the Reformation broke it had before it great possibilities. Already it had begun to incorporate the delicate craftsmanship of Italian sculptors, full of the new wine of the Early Renaissance, and had the world not been convulsed by a destructive revolution yet another page might have been added to the annals of Christian art, which did not die, but was incontinently slain, that a new era and a new art might come to birth.

After the anarchy and the awful destruction of the Reformation period had somewhat abated, and the new era begun, the old art was gone and something entirely new had taken its place. This is true at least of official art, the art of the new class of professional artists, of the constructive agencies in Church and State, of the new " upper classes " who were now completely differentiated from the (also new) proletariat. Amongst the peasantry and the country folk and the minor lords and squires the old fashion lingered on, and for a century or more the old ways held for the country churches (though few new ones were needed now), the cottages, and manors, and minor chateaux. It was a declining influence, however; little by little the peasantry lost their freedom, the squires and lords their independence, the priests their piety, the bishops and canons their intelligence, and by the end of the seventeenth century the last vestige of Mediæval art had disappeared. Will you have patience with me while I try to trace the circumstances of this great revolution?

When the spirit of the Middle Ages finally established itself throughout western Europe, the last traces of paganism had disappeared from religion, from philosophy, and from the social organism. The spirit of antiquity was that of obedience to nature and the worship of reason, with force as the *ultima ratio*. Its religion was the deification of the attributes of nature, from lust to power; its philosophy, the establishing of standards and the apprehension of absolute

truth through process of reason; the foundation of its society, slavery and the ar-
bitrament of physical force. This spirit of
antiquity which we call paganism had continued for five centuries after the Christian
Era, side by side with the new faith, and
though it had yielded here and there in religion and philosophy, it maintained itself
almost unhampered in the organization of
society, which was still definitely founded
on slavery. When the Empire broke down
in ruin, these partially submerged qualities
of paganism regained control of the West.
The first protest was on the instant, and at
the hands of St. Benedict, who led the revolt of those who were compelled to with-
draw from an intolerable world, under the
novel banner of Poverty, Chastity, Obedience, and Labour, the four antitheses to all
that paganism had held fundamental. For
five centuries, with most indifferent or
ephemeral results, Christianity strove to
establish its own principles over those of
paganism, and for the two following centuries it waged a warfare so successful that
in the end these principles stood supreme,
if not in universal action, at least in theoret-
ical acceptance. The spirit of antiquity had

declared that there was nothing higher than physical and human nature, except human reason, and that by the following of nature and reason men should become as gods. Christianity had preached a human nature corrupted by sin, but through the Incarnation and the Atonement glorified anew and subject to salvation through the grace of God, and explicitly by means of the ordained Sacraments of the Church. The two conceptions were built up on opposed bases and were different *in toto*. The Christian conception won, and for nearly five centuries determined the nature of religion, created an entirely new philosophy, and organized a society that had no prototype as it has had as yet no successor of like nature.

The five elements entering into the make-up of Mediævalism were: Northern blood, monasticism, the Catholic Faith, Sacramental philosophy, and the Christian commonwealth. It would be manifestly impossible to consider, even superficially, all these contributing causes, though all were operative in the production of the art we have been considering. While, however, the first four created the content of art and determined its indwelling spirit, it was the last that was chiefly instrumental in fixing the forms. Its complete destruction, within a brief space of years, had more than all else to do with the corresponding transformation of art from its Christian and Mediæval nature to its pagan and Renaissance (or modern) form. For this reason, and because the Christian commonwealth is little understood and generally misrepresented, I must speak of it, though as briefly as possible.

During the reconstruction of Europe after the fall of Rome, slavery tended, though by almost imperceptible degrees, to disappear. With the opening of the true Middle Ages its doom was sealed, and the fully developed Mediæval society founded itself on an entirely new basis. Slavery (domestic, industrial, and economic) had been the universal law of antiquity, a small group of individuals holding and controlling the land (that is to say, the chief means of production), together with all other forms of wealth and wealth-producing power. The vast majority of men existed by sufferance, without any personal means of production, and were maintained and permitted to breed simply because without their enforced labour the potential wealth in land, or other property, could not be made operative. Wives and children were chattels over whom the man frequently had the power of life and death, while over the labour, the persons, and the lives of the slaves the lord had almost unrestricted authority to do with them as he liked.

Under the Mediæval system the old Latin *villa,* or tract of land under the absolute ownership of a *dominus,* or lord, who worked it through his corps of slaves, had, through the process of feudalism, and by the ninth century, been wholly transformed. The estate was now divided into three portions, one the private property of the lord, one reserved to the tenants who practically though not as yet legally owned it, the third held for the common use of lord and yeomanry. By the twelfth century custom had determined the nature of the rent the peasant should pay his lord for use of the land, and what the lord was bound to render him in return, and by the fourteenth century peasant ownership was practically unquestioned. He could not be evicted from his land; it descended from father to son, and the rent paid either in kind or in money or in service was a small portion of the total possible income. This formed the tax the peasant paid; it was definite and limited, and no more in proportion to his income than the " State, county, town, and school tax " of today, let alone the question of indirect taxation of the innumerable kinds now in vogue. To put the case in a few words, the man on the land controlled the means of production, whereas both before Mediævalism and after the means of production were and are in the hands of a small group of landlords or capitalists.

Simultaneously trade and industry were developing along similar lines through the guilds. These were voluntary societies, covering all possible lines of activity, partly co-operative, but made up of private individuals owning and controlling their own means of production. Each body was self-governing, and it looked out for the education of the children of its members, gave aid and nursing in sickness, and burial at death. Above all it encouraged emulation amongst its members, but checked competition, guarded their rights and the scale of their wages, upheld the standards of workmanship, and jealously controlled the division of profits to prevent a great share falling into the hands of the few to the impoverishment of the many.

During the three great centuries of the central Middle Ages, there was neither slavery nor a division of society between a small group of capitalists (or owners of the means of production), on the one hand, and a vast proletariat made up of men dispossessed of the means of production on the other. Between the lord and the yeoman the difference was less of kind than of degree, while the priesthood, monasticism, and chivalry gave free and wide opportunities for ability to rise, as by a natural process, from one social scale to another, until it was no uncommon thing for a yeoman's son to become, on the one hand, page, squire, knight, baron, count; on the other, novice, monk, abbot, bishop, cardinal, and even Pope. If democracy consists, as it does, in abolition of privilege, and equal opportunity for all, then the Middle Ages form the only democracy of record, and if Catholicism had produced nothing else it deserves eternal honour for making this possible.

Through the guilds the same *" carrière*

ouverte aux talents" was made available, and ability alone determined whether the apprentice should remain such, or become the builder of Amiens or Rheims. Through the zealous guarding of standards, workmanship and artistic quality progressed steadily, and through co-operation a score of groups of independent artists and craftsmen worked in unison on the same building, with the same end in view, and with no quarrelling over precedence or the invasion of each other's territory. Is it any wonder that during the epoch of this only Christian commonwealth art should have flourished, and that Christian architecture should have been what it was?

Let us now consider the great revolution whereby the Middle Ages gave way to the Renaissance, Gothic to neo-classic, and Christianity to a revived paganism.

In the year 1250, the central moment of the Middle Ages, the Holy Roman Empire was dissolved. It was re-established in Germany alone, and Italy lost all effective and centralized government. From that moment anarchy began and came to its full estate as soon as the Papacy, the last centre of order, was removed to Avignon. No description could do justice to the carnival of profligacy and crime that reigned throughout Italy. Unscrupulous adventurers seized on power by force and fraud, extinguishing civil and moral rights and abandoning themselves to a career of treason, murder, treachery, poisoning, and almost inconceivable debauchery. All ethical standards were broken down; religion was derided, the authority of the Church in faith and morals was scorned and disregarded, and a complete return made to the spirit of antiquity, in that nature — human nature and reason — became the arbiter of conduct. All the hard-won liberties of the individual, the associations, and the communes disappeared in a pandemonium of tyranny. When this new spirit clothed itself with wealth, luxury, magnificence, art, and the patronage of letters, that it might hide its indelible bloodstains and extinguish by its glory all memory of its inconceivable crimes, Italy had become, as of old, a centre of omnipotent lords holding all power, all the means of production, with a vast proletariat, dispossessed, impoverished, and reduced to practical slavery.

The return to paganism in society and morals may have initiated, or it may simply have synchronized with, a corresponding return to pagan ideals in art. In any case the return was made, and in the midst of murder and outrage all Italy turned to the classical remains of letters, philosophy, and all the arts. The powerful vital force engendered by Mediævalism, at that very moment beginning there fully to express itself, was diverted into new channels, and an unexampled artistic splendour shone over the ruin of Christian society and the inauguration of the new paganism; palliating its crimes and almost justifying its pretensions.

From Italy this enthralling new spirit extended itself little by little over all Europe. It came, as it could, in fascinating form; and on the strength of its art, its new learning, its lavish splendour, found ready acceptance. At once, however, its poison began to work, — in society, in philosophy, and in religion. By this time the Church itself, almost wholly in Italy, increasingly in France and Germany, had made its surrender, and the power the first of the new pagans fought furiously because of its stand for Christian morals and Christian faith, was now their fellow and accessory. The monasteries held out longest against the insanity of fundamental humanism, some of them successfully, but their influence became less and less, and finally almost negligible.

The pagan revolution in Italy resulted in the temporary abandonment of Christian faith and morals, and in the acquisition of all the wealth and the means of production by a group of omnipotent assassins. In France, while religion still held a formal supremacy, its effectiveness was appallingly diminished, morals degenerated, though less fatally than in the south, but the social revolution was quite as complete and resulted through the Wars of Religion in an equal extinguishing of Mediæval liberty and the mingling in the crown of all power, all authority, and an enormous area of territory from which the new proletariat had been dispossessed.

In England the Renaissance came slowly, so far as its æsthetic and literary amenities are concerned, and its religious and philosophical corollaries as well. Curiously enough, however, the economic revolution made its way more rapidly. In the early fifteenth century the great mass of Englishmen owned the land on which they lived and laboured, and all other means of production as well. Wealth was distributed with a close approach to evenness, and was more abundant than in any other part of Europe. The greatest landlord was the Church, holding something over a quarter of the land, but the taxes (or rents) were low, collected with unbusinesslike leniency, and largely established by immemorial custom and therefore subject to little change. By the beginning of the sixteenth century the group of landholders had begun to increase their holdings, while the small owners were diminishing in number. There was little as yet that was alarming in the change, which might easily have been arrested, but at this critical moment occurred the greatest economic disaster England has ever known, the suppression of the monasteries, and the giving over of their vast lands to the cabal of new and needy and greedy nobles who had been called (and who had paid) to take the place of the men of old honour who had fallen during the Wars of the Roses. A fourth of the wealth-

producing land of England was at a blow
handed over to a very sorry group of knaves
and sycophants, mostly of inferior blood:
tenants by tens of thousands were dispossessed and driven out to starve or turn outlaw, and in ten years England had ceased
to be a Commonwealth, and had become, as
Italy and France, a nation made up of a
land-owning and wealth-controlling minority on the one hand, a proletarian and help-
less and poverty-stricken majority on the
other.

In a century the whole social fabric of
Europe had been revolutionized, and the
Mediæval system of an approximate equal-
ity in landholding, in possession of the
means of production, and in the distribution of wealth (and therefore in opportunity), had given place to the Capitalistic
State, consisting of an absolute and ever-
increasing inequality in all these elements
that form the only foundation for a just and
righteous commonwealth.

Meanwhile another series of catastrophies
had overtaken Europe in the shape of certain great wars which marked the rise and
progress of the Renaissance and Reformation, wars compared with which the mili-

tary expeditions of Mediævalism were mere skirmishes. Their results were equally unlike, and of a most fatal nature. During Mediævalism the nobility in every Christian country of Europe was of pure northern stock, tracing its lineage back to the hardy lands around the Baltic. So was the great mass of the people, except in Spain, southern France, and the lower half of Italy, but underneath was always a substratum of the round-headed Alpine race of which the present southern Slavs are a part, with, in the south, a debased mixture of many servile strains. The Crusades and the wars of Mediævalism had cut into the noble and peasant classes of northern blood in about equal proportions, but now something very different was to occur, and this was a series of wide and long-drawn-out conflicts in which the men of the purest blood and best traditions and highest mentality were practically exterminated.

The Wars of the Roses, the Thirty Years' War in Germany, the Wars of Religion in France and Flanders, and, later, the religious persecutions in England, with the wars of the Commonwealth, struck primarily at the class of nobles, knights, and gentlemen, and secondarily at the yeomanry of northern blood, so planing away all the wonderful superstructure of culture, character, and chivalry, and releasing the lowest strata of all, which came swiftly to the top, and, with no traditions of culture, character, or chivalry, assumed to fill the depleted ranks.

Of the Thirty Years' War in Germany and its results on the race and society, Madison Grant says:

"It destroyed an entire generation, taking each year for thirty years the finest manhood of the nation. Two-thirds of the population of Germany was destroyed in some states, such as Bohemia; while out of 500,000 people in Württemberg there were only 48,000 left at the end of the war. . . . From that time on the purely Teutonic race in Germany has been largely replaced by the Alpine type in the south and the Wendish and Polish types in the east. . . . Out of 70,000,000 inhabitants of the German Empire only 9,000,000 are purely Teutonic. . . . In addition the Thirty Years' War virtually destroyed the land-owning yeomanry and lesser gentry formerly found in Germany as numerously as in France or in

England. . . . This section of the population was largely exterminated, and the class of gentlemen practically vanishes from German history from that time on. When the Thirty Years' War was over there remained in Germany nothing except the brutalized peasantry, and the high nobility which turned from the toils of endless warfare to mimic on a small scale the Court of Versailles. Today the ghastly rarity in the German armies of chivalry and generosity toward women and of knightly protection and courtesy toward the prisoners and wounded can be largely attributed to this annihilation of the gentle class. The Germans of today, whether they live on the farms or in the cities, are for the most part descendants of the peasants who survived, not of the brilliant knights and hardy foot soldiers who fell in that mighty conflict."

The result of the wars of the fifteenth, the sixteenth, and the seventeenth centuries in France and England was less terribly comprehensive, but the same in nature. All the fine flower of Mediæval culture was swept away; debased and adulterated stock came to the surface and ruthlessly gathered the power and the means of production into its own hands. The hold of religion was gone, the monasteries suppressed, the customs and relationships of feudal society superseded by force and by class legislation, and at the very moment of complete success came the great industrial discoveries of coal and iron as potentialities of wealth, whose infinite possibilities had been unlocked by the solving of the problem of steam as manageable energy. One invention followed another, with endless new discoveries, each of which might be given an industrial application. The proletariat, made out of the free citizens of a dead Mediævalism, could not use them, but the new class of capitalists made out of the up springing dregs of a dead civilization, could and did, now that all restraining influences had been removed, and since they were the holders of all wealth and all wealth-producing agencies. The result was Industrial Civilization, of which Alfred Russell Wallace could write, in the year before the War:

" It is not too much to say that our whole system of society is rotten from top to bottom, and the Social Environment as a whole, in relation to our possibilities and our claims, is the worst that the world has ever seen."

I have called this, my last lecture, "The Decadence and the New Paganism." I have apologized for using the word "decadence" as applied to the latest architecture of Mediævalism, but I have no apologies to make for applying the words "new paganism" to the scheme of life that took the place of that of the great five centuries of Christian civilization. Do not misunderstand me: I do not claim for Mediæval society any degree of perfection. The most constructive student of the time America has yet produced, Henry Osborne Taylor, has written of what he calls "the spotted actuality." It *was* "spotted," mingled of good and evil, as are all peoples, all generations, all men, and as these must be mingled of good and evil for all time. I do declare the thesis, however, that it was a time when the principles of Christianity were the dominant and controlling force, and when the "spotted actuality" contained a greater proportion of good than has been recorded in history either before or since.

The new paganism was in religion, in philosophy, in sociology, in economics, in ethics, and in art, a definite and categorical return to the old paganism. It is argued, and may be debatable, that such a return was an evidence of human evolution toward something higher and more wholesome than Christianity could afford. It may be so, but the eternal antithesis must be recognized and men must now admit that society can no longer continue half Christian and half pagan. With more than exemplary patience Christianity has surrendered one position after another in the vain effort to affect a compromise and maintain a working basis with the universal force that re-entered the world just five centuries ago. The result is now for us to see in the elapsed years of the twentieth century, made clear and unmistakable by the events that have cast the red light of their apocalyptic revelation over the delusive present, ever since the first day of August in the year of Our Lord, One Thousand Nine Hundred and Fourteen.

There remain for us only a few words as to the workings of this new paganism in the architecture that in seven centuries had grown from the hesitating efforts of Charlemagne's clumsy builders to the awful majesty of Chartres, the kindly and human and beautiful Lincoln, the serene consummation of Rheims. It was at first a stimulus, for the high ardour of Mediævalism was still there, and it used the delicacy and the craft and the pleasant fancy of the earliest Renaissance to give a new charm to its own imaginings. Then came the division of society between capitalist and proletarian, the concentration of wealth and the means to wealth in a few hands, the dissolution of the guilds, the suppression of the monasteries, the restoration of tyranny and absolutism in government, the moral apostasy of the Church. Intellectualism took the place of conscience and Revelation; individualism destroyed liberty and co-operation, and all the mainsprings of communal art were dried up.

For the art of the Middle Ages was a communal art, and in this may lie the secret of its character. It grew from the spontaneous demand of a whole people under the influence of a great and vital impulse. No beneficent millionaire, no Brahmin of superior taste, no august and official academy, no suddenly enriched middle class with social ambitions gave the call or dictated the forms or the fashions they would patronize. There were no architects as such, and no contractors; no vast and efficient building organizations on the one hand, or industrious walking delegates on the other. No man stood by himself on a pinnacle of superiority and by competitive bids chose the cheapest workmen, dictated to them what they should do, and, subject to the veto of the labour unions, saw that they did it. Mediæval architecture was the work of free, proud, independent artists and craftsmen, working together, each in his own sphere, and all to the common end of producing something better and more beautiful than had ever been seen before.

The moment the Early Renaissance became the Pagan Renaissance, all this was changed. The new art was the appanage of the specialist: the people as a whole did not like it or want it, the craftsmen knew nothing about it and cared less. From its very nature it excluded personal artistry and individual initiative, and nothing remained, if the work was to be accomplished, but the invention of the architect. He was invented out of the amateurs and dilettanti of the literary circles of Italy and began his career of designing, controlling, directing every branch of an art that in its great days was not the result of an æsthetic fiat, but of the co-operation of as many artists as there were arts, as many craftsmen as there were crafts. The guilds dissolved, craftsmanship died of disuse, classical details, carefully drawn for day labourers to cut, worked their way fantastically into the lingering Gothic compositions, crowded them out, and established themselves as the exclusive claimants to the admiration of the elect.

And still the old inheritance of good taste and the love of beauty and joy in craftsmanship lingered here and there: the real and fine principles of the old classic architecture worked through the silly admiration of superficial forms and built up a new style that often reached levels of great majesty and distinguished beauty. But it was now a new style, and could only be this in common honesty, for the life and thought to which it gave expression were equally new. It is inconceivable that the art of the Middle Ages could have continued to voice the Renaissance, the Reformation, and the Revolution, and to give outward shape to

the spirit of the Capitalistic and Industrial
State which is the synthesis of these, the
solar plexus of modernism. Gothic art had
done its work; it had given immortal form
to Christian civilization, and it passed with
the splendid thing it had so faithfully
served. It can never come back, at least
with the life and power that were its own.
Haltingly restored it may serve well as the
visible protest of the Church and the university against their eternal enemy, the new
paganism. Whether its *spirit* comes back,
to express, in some new series of forms, the
righteous and eternal forces that made the
Mediæval man and the Mediæval State,
depends on the answer the world gives to
the great question propounded by the War.

We have had our chance and have made
of it — what we have made. Modern civilization has now reached that impasse from
which the way of escape is apparently by
way of war. Revolution follows close; it
may be that the war itself will merge in
revolution with no military termination that
finds its position in a treaty of peace, while
the inevitable process of overturning the
entire economic and industrial basis of society supersedes a war of armed forces and

[199]

brings in the more terrible contest of classes and of systems. No prediction is plausible except that, whether now or later, the revolution is not to be escaped and that in the end all we have known as modern civilization will have passed and a new era have come into being.

The new paganism has had its era of five centuries and no definite epoch has ever lasted beyond this period. The end is very close at hand; whether the next step is into five centuries of Dark Ages or into a new era of five centuries of a restored Christian commonwealth, depends on us. The choice is free; we are not constrained in our decision, but on that decision hangs the happiness or misery, the honour or the shame, the righteousness or the apostasy of the world. Men rejected Christian civilization for the new paganism once, when the choice was offered them. Will they now in turn reject their former choice that the Christian commonwealth may be restored?